D1407885

Dear Mike,

We hope you enjoy our book and benefit by having a better understanding of how annuities can help solve some of the serious challenges facing today's retirees.

Best Wishes on your Successful Retirement!

Annuity Guys,

Dick and Eric

Retirement Educators

If you benefit from this Annuity Reference Book, please let others know by giving your opinion in a review at Amazon.com.

Send an email to retirewell@dvdfinancial.com if you have any questions about retirement, annuities, or suggestions on how this book might be improved.

Forward

"Seek first to understand, then to be understood."

Stephen R. Covey

As financial advisors, we are constantly pressed with maintaining an understanding of the economic landscape and products used to navigate the financial world. Some advisors are pioneers while others choose to follow the trail once it has become well traveled. Sometimes those of us who choose to cut a path away from the well-traveled road are derided by our peers who fail to understand the potential of a strategy or system--only to be hailed in time as trailblazers when our vision becomes truly understood by the masses. Annuity allocations, in a balanced portfolio are just such a topic as this has now moved into the mainstream of today's retirement planning.

The New Retirement lays out a foundation that will empower readers to:

- Know if an annuity may be suitable for one's portfolio;
- Understand the differing types of annuities;
- Learn different annuity strategies for unique situations;
- Comprehend the pros and cons of all annuities;
- Know the difference between facts and fiction about annuities.

As more and more clients have been forced into 401k plans and away from employer pension programs, annuities have taken on a much larger role in financial asset allocations. We recommend working with a financial advisor who will take the time to understand your goals and needs and then will work to assist you in creating a financial plan that will allow for a comfortable, secure retirement.

We hope you find a great value, as many others have, when you digest these pages and that this book assists you to achieve peace of mind and the comfort of financial security in retirement.

Sincerely,

Eric

Disclosure

THE NEW RETIREMENT: A PARADIGM SHIFT

Table of Contents

Forward 2

Disclosure 3

Preface 11

Introduction 12

Book Terms and Definitions.......................... 13

Chapter 1: Uncharted Territory............................ 16

The Retirement Challenges We Face 18

Live Long and Prosper! 23

Retirement Obstacles to Prepare For...................... 24

Video: What is Your Retirement Strategy................... 28

Chapter 2: All Advisors are the Same, NOT!.............. 29

Case Study 1 -- Jill 30

Financial Advisors with Divided Interests! 30

Choosing an Advisor 31

Financial Advisor Titles & Descriptions 33

Professional Designations 35

It's Time to Decide on an Advisor!......................... 37

How Financial Advisors Are Regulated..................... 37

Questions to Ask a Prospective Advisor.................... 38

Subjects an Advisor Should Ask About 41

The Client's Responsibilities 41

Video: Avoiding a Bad Advisor Experience 43

Chapter 3: Annuities -- Not Created Equal! 44

Case Study 2 -- Jane 45

Understanding Annuities 46

Different Types of Annuities................................. 47

Choosing an Annuity 53

Video: What is The Best Annuity?.. 56

Chapter 4: MarketFree™ Fixed Annuities 57

Case Study 3 -- Jan and Steve... 58

The History of Fixed Annuities 59

Fact or Fiction - Know the Truth! 60

MarketFree™ Fixed Annuities & Retirement 63

Fixed Annuity Characteristics 65

Fixed Annuity Benefits.. 65

Fixed Annuity Performance... 65

Fixed Deferred Annuities.. 66

Fixed Deferred Annuity Characteristics 67

MarketFree™ Fixed Annuity -- CD-Style................................... 67

Fixed Annuity Alternatives... 69

Fixed Annuity Disadvantages 70

Choosing the Best Fixed Annuity.. 71

Video: MarketFree™ Fixed Annuities Advisors Love or Hate Them 74

Chapter 5: Variable Annuities... 75

Case Study 4 -- Jim.. 76

Variable Annuity History 76

All Annuities are Variable -- Right?... 77

Fact or Fiction - Know the Truth! 78

Variable Annuity Features 80

Variable Annuity Benefits 81

Variable Annuity Performance 81

Variable Annuity Alternatives 82

Variable Annuity Disadvantages... 83

Choosing the Best Variable Annuities 83

Video: Variable Annuity vs. Hybrid Annuity 85

Chapter 6: 86

MarketFree™ Fixed Index Annuities 86

Case Study 5 -- Mike and Lisa 87

Fixed Index Annuity History 87

Understanding Fixed Index Annuities (FIA) 88

Fact or Fiction - Know the Truth! 89

Fixed Index Annuity Features 91

Fixed Index Annuity Benefits... 93

Income Riders & Contractual Guarantees -"Absolute guarantees, No-moving parts."... 93

MarketFree™ Index Annuity Specifics 93

Index Strategy Moving Parts 94

Index Strategies & Various Time Period... 97

Index Annuity Performance... 97

Fixed Index Annuity Disadvantages... 97

Choosing a Fixed Index Annuity 98

Video: Fixed Index Annuity Choices 100

Chapter 7: 101

MarketFree™ Life Immediate Annuities.................................... 101

Case Study 6 -- Sarah 102

Understanding Life Immediate Annuities.................................... 102

Fact or Fiction...Know the Truth! 103

Immediate Annuity Options... 105

Other Types of Immediate Annuities.. 107

Immediate Annuity Benefits... 108

Immediate Annuity Performance 110

Immediate Annuity Disadvantages... 110

Choosing a Immediate Annuity... 112

Video: New Immediate Hybrid Annuities................................ 113

Chapter 8: MarketFree™ Hybrid Annuities 114

Case Study 7 -- Bob 115

Understanding Hybrid Annuities 116

Fact or Fiction... Know the Truth! 116

Hybrid Annuity Features 118

Hybrid Annuity Benefits 121

Index Riders & Contractual Guarantees 122

Hybrid Annuity Specifics 122

Hybrid Index Strategy Moving Parts 123

Index Strategies & Various Time Periods................................ 125

Choosing a Hybrid Annuity 126

Hybrid Annuity Disadvantages... 126

Video: MarketFree™ Hybrid Annuities.................................. 128

Chapter 9: Annuity Riders.. 129

Case Study 8 -- Teresa and Ann 130

Understanding Annuity Riders.. 130

Death Benefit Riders... 131

Types of Death Benefit Riders 133

Living Benefit Riders... 134

Types of Living Benefit Riders 136

When Are Living Benefits Riders Right?................................. 139

Long-Term Care Rider 141

Increasing Income Payout Rider 141

How Most Annuity Income Riders Work 143

Video: Who Needs an Income Rider? 144

Chapter 10: Annuity Discussions 145

Case Study 9 -- Jack and Mary 146

Video: The Five Top Annuity Safety Risks 147

Are Annuities Safe? 148

Video: High Annuity Rates or Ratings? 152

Annuity Satisfaction 153

Annuities and Retirement 153

Annuities and Tax 154

Annuities & Estate Tax 160

Video: Annuities & Estate Planning 161

Rollovers & Annuities 162

Video: Avoid Tax On IRA & 401K Rollovers! 164

FIAs & Hybrids: Buy-or-Beware 165

Video: Top Ten Hybrid Annuity Questions 169

Understanding MarketFree Pre-Issued Annuities™ 170

Positive Attributes - Pre-Issued Annuities™ 170

Negative Attributes - Pre-Issued Annuities™ 170

Pre-Issued Annuity™ Safety & Yield 171

Pre-Issued Annuity™ Experts 172

Pre-Issued Annuity™ Advantages 172

Pre-Issued Annuity™ Disadvantages 172

Pre-Issued Annuity ™ vs. Hybrid Annuity 173

Pre-Issued Annuity ™ and Hybrid Annuity 173

Shared Advantages 173

Pre-Issued Annuity™ and Hybrid Annuity and Shared Disadvantages .. 174

Video: Pre Issued Annuities™ Safety & Yield 175

Chapter 11: Advisor Ethics and Standards............................... 176

Case Study 10 -- Tim and Martha 177

Ethics for Advisors... 177

Required Code of Ethics for Advisors 180

Video: Finding a Great Retirement Advisor............................... 182

Chapter 12: SEC & FINRA - Friend or Foe? 183

Case Study 11 -- Robert and Sarah 184

Insurance and Investment Regulation....................................... 184

Securities and Exchange Commission (SEC).............................. 185

Financial Industry Regulatory Authority 187

(FINRA) 187

Check Out Brokers & Investment Advisors 188

Avoiding Scams.. 190

Other Sources for Investor Education and Safety....................... 192

Recognizing Scammers 194

Video: Is it Crazy or Smart to Work with an Internet Specialist 197

Chapter 13: Some Annuities Are Ugly! 198

UGLY Annuities 198

Market Free™ Annuities Unfairly Attacked................................ 199

Video: The Too Good to Be True 8 Percent Annuity Return Secret ... 203

Chapter 14: Is Social Security an Annuity? 204

Should Social Security be Relied On? 205

Negative Press Gets Attention 205

Social Security's Impact On US Citizens 206

Is Social Security the Ultimate Annuity?................................... 208

Understanding Social Security... 208

Summary 212

Video: Social Security is it Considered to be the Ultimate Annuity? .. 213

Annuity/Financial Glossary 215

INDEX 240

Further Disclosure 250

Preface

The New Retirement: A Paradigm Shift began out of a desire to pull years of experience and research together for the present retirement crisis. Annuity Guys have made these resources available and shared them on an individual basis over the course of some years as multi-disciplinary retirement advisors and financial planners.

Over time, we have written and compiled hundreds of pages of information for newsletters, websites, retirement seminars, and client letters.

Use this book as a reference guide or field book, study what you need more knowledge on. Utilize it as needed for learning more about retirement planning and the many different types of annuities and allocation strategies that exist. This book was not written to be read like a novel, from cover to cover, although many do choose to read it that way.

In addition, we have enjoyed the shared experiences of discussing firsthand investment and annuity experiences with hundreds of individuals-- some experiences were; good, bad, and some yes, ugly!

Through the pages of this book, we have woven our professional and personal experiences involving some real-life examples from our financial practice experience. It is our hope that this helps bring the reality of making good financial decisions to life for each reader, making for enjoyable yet informative reading.

The names and exact details have been changed to protect individual identities and all confidential financial information.

So read, learn, enjoy, and apply when appropriate.

Introduction

As the Annuity Guys, being somewhat frustrated with so many misstatements, half truths, and a few outright lies about financial strategies in general--and annuities more specifically--we have decided to apply our knowledge based on experience and led by our inner compass to right the record. The question that may be going through one's mind at this moment and one we have wrestled with is simply with so much bias and half-truth - "Can one book have any real impact? Is it worth the effort?"

Well, let us think about this for a moment. We remember a story about a little girl walking along the seashore with her daddy after the tide had just gone out. There were starfish everywhere and the little girl kept interrupting her father's walk by stopping to place starfish back into the sea. Her father, becoming somewhat annoyed, pointed out to his young daughter that there were hundreds of starfish as far as the eye could see and that it was an impossible task. He was hoping that she would see the futility and agree with him so they could start walking steadily again. He then asked her if what she was doing would really matter or makes any real difference. Her answer was innocently spoken as she said, "It makes a difference to this one, Daddy." She gently set her next starfish back in the sea.

We do not pretend to answer with the innocence or profoundness of this young girl. However, this is the essence of why we wrote this book. We have seen many times the substantial benefits of our friends, clients, and family receiving and implementing great financial advice.

Please accept this book as a sincere attempt to help readers who have crossed our path.

Book Terms and Definitions

This book can only be understood correctly based on the definitions of these terms:

Account - any place actual money is held

Allocations - various places for money which also includes annuities

Annuitization - when income is guaranteed by an insurance company in return for forfeiting principal/premium or/and account value over to the control of the insurance company with no future access of funds by the client other than contractually guaranteed income

Bonus - money paid by any financial institution to gain your business

Cash Account - where actual money held with growth potential and withdrawal privileges

Contractual Guarantee - any financial contract guaranteeing growth of principal, income or some other monetary benefit

Deposits - money placed in any financial vehicle

Diversification - different places for individuals to place money

FDIC - **Guarantees Bank Accounts Only,** *Annuities are guaranteed by the claims paying ability of the issuing insurance company*

Fees - any charge against account value regardless of no growth, gain or loss

Fixed Annuity - Any annuity that guarantees initial principal/premium and future account value **having NO investment risk**--offering various interest earning strategies

Hybrid Annuity - is simply *a fixed annuity* offering both a specified rate of interest or a market linked index option(s)-- for greater potential interest earnings, and a lifetime pay option that does not force annuitization

Immediate Annuity - when income is guaranteed by an insurance company in return for a lump sum of principal/premium paid to the insurance company with no future access of funds by the client other than a set contractually guaranteed income on fixed immediate annuities and a fluctuating lifetime income on variable immediate annuities

Income Account - a non-monetary annuity account that has contractually guaranteed growth to produce a minimum contractually guaranteed future income

Income Floor - the minimum income produced regardless of economic conditions as a safety-net in annuities

Investment - any non-insurance financial vehicle with the exception of variable annuities and variable life insurance

Investors - individuals in general

Majority Control - maintaining ownership and access to about 90 percent of initial annuity principal/premium allocated to an annuity even in a worst case full surrender scenario; annuities have declining surrenders which increase majority control to 100 percent of initial principal/premium/account value at annuity maturity

MarketFree™ - market risk free, having no stock, bond, commodity, or securities market risk, safe money financial instruments that are not securities that do not subject principal or gains to losses based on any market fluctuations a.k.a. *MarketFree*™ *Annuities, Annuity, Retirement(s), Portfolio(s) etc.*

MarketFree™ *Annuities* - all annuities or portfolios of annuities that protect principal or premium and growth by remaining market risk free

Non-MarketFree™ *Annuities* – variable annuities

Maturity - When annuity surrender charges or penalties end--offering owners full liquidity; insurers still have to maintain all contractual obligations after maturity--lasting throughout the annuity owners lifetime

Portfolio - all assets held by an individual

Premium - money placed into insurance contracts

Principal - money placed into any financial instrument or any verifiable account value

Spread - any charge that is only invoked with a corresponding gain in account value

SIGA - State Insurance Guarantee Associations-- vary in coverage with each state and are **not to be confused with FDIC which has the backing of the federal government**

Variable Annuity - Any annuity that does not guarantee the owners initial principal/premium or future account value while living **and owners typically assume ALL market risk**—typically offers various sub-account investment options, classified and regulated as insurance and a securities financial instrument, may offer various death benefits to offset market losses, not a MarketFree™ Annuity

Chapter 1: Uncharted Territory

"I used to let someone else do my investing. Now, as you can see, I am taking less risk with no vidersification."

"Money is like a sixth sense - and you can't make use of the other five without it." - William Somerset Maugham

Throughout history, each generation has had its challenges and today it is no different. Even with the constant advances made in technology, travel, medicine, and the interconnected economies of the world at large, there are many new hurdles especially for retirees to overcome.

Today, more than ever before, we face retirement challenges that are far different than what our parents or our grandparents faced. Not too many years ago, a faithful employee could work his or her entire career for one employer and in return receive a nice pension as well as health insurance benefits that would last for the remainder of his or her life. Those days are quickly becoming a distant memory and the responsibility for ensuring that there is enough income in retirement is mostly up to just one person now-- **YOU.**

Taking on this responsibility can be daunting for employees. Many companies offer retirement savings plans such as a 401(k) yet employees for the most part have no idea how much will be needed in retirement--and thus have no idea how much money needs to be put away for retirement. For those retirees who have accumulated sizeable retirement assets, it is also challenging in our present economic uncertainty to develop a plan that gives the assurance that those assets will provide needed income lasting for twenty to thirty years or so of retirement without running out of money.

Coupled with this uncertainty, the possibility of running out of money is a serious concern. Many investors have seen the value of retirement savings drop considerably over the past several years making it even more difficult to know how to catch up or get back on track with any type of retirement growth initiatives.

The bottom line is that the responsibility of providing for retirement income and the determination of a retirement lifestyle is up to each individual. So knowing how to plan properly can prepare a person for living the pleasant retirement dreamed of without it becoming more like a nightmare. It is also necessary to know just how much individual retirees can actually spend throughout retirement years without feeling false guilt about overspending or unnecessary fearful thoughts that the money may not last.

Many factors have led to a substantial paradigm shift for retirees that have sent individuals in search of financial solutions which offer security in retirement since the past successes of many, buying and holding stocks and bonds have now lost considerable value and destroyed several retirement plans without warning.

MarketFree™ annuities are in no way a panacea or a silver bullet; however they continually prove to be a wise choice for many retirees when added to a portfolio as a foundational asset class in place of bonds or banking instruments for the fixed-income portion of a well-balanced retirement portfolio.

The Retirement Challenges We Face

In the past, most U.S. employees were much more confident about their ability to live comfortably throughout retirement years. Employees felt safe saving and investing a certain amount each month from his or her paycheck over a certain number of years. This is because savings were typically only part of retirement security--the rest was enhanced by an employer's pension plan along with income from Social Security.

But today, this is simply not the case for most folks. There are numerous threats facing retirement savings, investment uncertainty, lack of pensions and even an endangered Social Security system. These factors aren't something we simply hear about in the news; these factors are real and present concerns that have a huge impact on how retirees are able to survive or thrive in the future.

Many experts today believe that based on current United States deficits exponentially compounded by unsustainable entitlement programs, an increased regulatory climate, and debt-heavy struggling world economies, we may be in for another rough decade or two when it comes to the economy--and especially when it comes to *sustainable* stock market returns.

Some of the primary challenges we face that can negatively impact retirement assets and income include:

Low Interest Rates

Low interest earnings in "safe" accounts such as bank CDs, investment-grade bonds, and certain fixed annuities historically have not kept pace with inflation. Compounding the problem even further is the fact that many of these retirement income vehicles are offering the lowest interest rates seen in U.S. history.

Investment Risk

The first decade of the twenty-first century--known as the lost decade--gave us a rollercoaster stock market that went no-where. The returns for most investors were flat during this time period and many investors who invested their entire retirement portfolios into the market are now staying away completely, that is, if they still have much left to invest after pulling out when markets were plummeting.

Remaining in market investment risk has never been considered a secure or foundational place for reliable income that may need to last for two or more decades in retirement.

Broken Fiscal Policy

With regard to U.S. fiscal policy, the amount of on-budget federal debt held by US citizens and foreign governments now exceeds 100 percent of annual GDP, and off-budget debt (future entitlement commitments) may well exceed 300 to 400 percent - all while prospective debt dynamics continue to worsen significantly. The on-budget debt level has not been this high since just after World War II. The off-budget debt is unprecedented. Without some type of major political compromise the debt will likely keep rising until a resulting financial crisis arises or it becomes politically expedient for some other reason to solve the debt issue.

Certainly, the challenges that are currently facing the financial solvency of the United States should not be underestimated, especially given the economic headwinds facing the private sector with the prospect of large spending increases, an aging population- needing Social Security, and health care entitlement benefits, all adding to the current debt.

World Economies Imploding with Debt

Many countries throughout the world have borrowed and increased debt to such a high level that they are facing a danger of their economies collapsing. Many investments that retirement accounts are allocated to can be either directly or indirectly affected in a negative way by faltering world economies. Many European nations and the United States have made headlines recently with actual and potential credit rating downgrades.

The United States dollar is used in a great many international transactions as the world currency standard. It stands to reason that just about anything that happens to the economy in the U.S. will also have a substantial effect on international finance. For example, when the Federal Reserve Bank (Fed) raises interest rates, the foreign exchange value of the dollar will typically go up as well. Conversely, the value of the dollar is normally suppressed when rates are kept low.

With the dollar devalued, many of the countries that export goods to the United States can have a reduction in demand for their products. And those nations that have reduced exports could actually suffer some dramatic consequences due to this type of downturn in U.S. spending. This, in turn, can cause these countries to be less capable of purchasing U.S. exports which will further enhance a downward spiral. As a result, there are a number of countries that could lose a great deal if the U.S. were to keep devaluing its dollar or remain in a prolonged recession or a sluggish economic recovery.

The world economy is complex and interconnected in such a way that the risks are ever present as governments continue to spend irresponsibly in epidemic proportions. When the exact corrective turning point is or when a day of reckoning will happen is anyone's guess; the world at large is drowning in debt and real change is continually pushed further down the road.

Retirement Accounts = Tax Time Bomb

Retirees who begin withdrawing funds from retirement plans such as an IRA or 401(K) will have income tax to pay on all of those dollars which is expensive at today's tax rates and likely to increase even more in the future. It is important to minimize, where possible, the income and estate tax that will be levied against retirees' income, savings and wealth transferred to heirs.

If proper estate and income strategies during retirement are not correctly utilized, many retirees are at risk of losing nearly half or more of his or her present assets to excessive draconian estate taxation without even considering any future tax increases.

Long-Term Care Uncertainty

The cost of needing long-term care, whether in a facility or at home continues to increase each year. Overall, the approximate nationwide average daily cost for a semi-private room in a skilled nursing facility in 2010 was $205 per day, and the average daily cost of a private room was $229. This equates to nearly $75,000 to $85,000 per year respectively.

Long-term care insurers are now raising rates dramatically. With these costs spiraling out of control and fewer people opting to purchase policies, there is constant upward pressure on rates making long-term care insurance likely to be unaffordable for many.

Retirees who have not properly prepared for these potential costs have a major retirement portfolio vulnerability, especially if one spouse needs care while the other is still at home and responsible for all of the regular living expenses of maintaining a standard of living.

Market Volatility & Perhaps another Lost Decade or Two

Over time, there have been distinct periods of bull markets and bear markets. Since 1999, as a recent example, we have experienced extreme volatility in the markets. Because of this, investing for the future--especially in or near retirement--may need to be more tactical in order to not only gain but also to retain and protect those gains to reduce or eliminate the risk of principal loss and the loss of ongoing earnings.

Tax-Hungry Politicians & Bureaucrats

It is good to be proactive and be aware of how much income and retirement funds are being taxed or may be taxed in the future. It may be nearly impossible to control our runaway government spending thus it is imperative to be aware of the taxes that are currently levied and future tax that may be coming soon.

Now, it is more important than ever before to become proactive in reducing the amount that is paid in tax individually and to do more tax advantaged planning for secure retirements which may need to span a few decades.

Destabilizing U.S. Debt

In addition to protecting retirement savings and taking a proactive role in lowering taxes, there are a number of factors that we have absolutely no control over that can still greatly affect our retirement savings and ultimately our retirement lifestyles.

The current U.S. deficit and debt which continues to grow can eventually have a substantial negative impact on retirees in the future. One such example of how this could happen is with the potential budget deficit reduction proposals to help save Medicare and Social Security. Here we could begin to see cuts in Medicare and Social Security benefits which, even with the best of intentions, would have a negative effect on millions of retirees.

Supersized Inflation Likely

Inflation is actually caused by a devaluation of a nation's currency. The United States dollar has been in a position of prestige and considered to be the worldwide standard. However, over time, the depreciation of the U.S. dollar has been directly connected to our increasing national debt and the U.S. remaining as the world currency standard is now openly being debated by other countries.

When the Fed buys government debt and prints or digitally creates more money in order to cover its new debt, the dollar loses value. And recently the Fed has been expanding the money supply by historic and unprecedented proportions thus setting the stage potentially for hyper-inflation. Many experts seem to agree that the stage is set for higher inflation over the next two or three decades. In fact, from 1971 through 2011, inflation has been over the 4 percent mark. Certainly, an increase in the general level of prices will substantially reduce the purchasing power of retirees on fixed incomes.

Since many retirees live on fixed incomes, it could become difficult in this present low-interest-rate environment to keep retirement income up to speed with inflation while still maintaining a high degree of safety for ones income.

Health Care Skyrocketing

Each year, we hear more and more about higher health care costs and nowhere is this more of a concern than for retirees--most of whom no longer have comprehensive health care coverage from former employers. The Affordable

Unfortunately, these skyrocketing health care costs are not just going through a temporary upward cycle. Statistics show that the cost of health care has outpaced the rate of inflation for individuals over the past twenty years and these prices are projected to continually increase as much as 10-15 percent annually. At that rate, retirees could expect to see health care costs double in about ten years or less.

Litigation Threats

Regardless of how safe and secure retirees may feel, there is always the possibility that his or her hard-earned assets could end up in someone else's pocket. No matter what the profession or status in life, we live in a very litigious society; therefore lawsuits are a real possibility and cannot be ruled out.

Any loss of assets will cause a corresponding threat to an estate value or present retirement income, so positioning assets for protection against litigation is vital. Yet, until it happens, most may not realize just how vulnerable retirement assets and future retirement income truly are.

Live Long and Prosper!

Most of us certainly strive to live a nice long and healthy life. However, the irony of this is that retirees nowadays are often finding themselves concerned about the financial risk of living or outliving a normal life expectancy. And some retirees who are living longer, but not necessarily healthier, are facing even more financial hardships trying to cope with paying additional health care or long-term care expenses in addition to normal daily living costs in retirement.

Back in 1900, at the turn of the twentieth century, the average life expectancy was approximately forty-seven years. Today, forty-seven is considered to be middle age--in fact, it is considered to be quite young relative to retirement age for most. Many people today are just starting families or running marathons at age forty and beyond!

Presently, the average life expectancy for a male is just over seventy-six years. And a female child born today in the U.S. will have a life expectancy of over eighty-one years. So what does this mean with regard to planning for the future?

It means that people could live in retirement for twenty to forty years; that not only must people plan and save before retirement, one must also follow a well-thought-out retirement plan in order to stretch those retirement dollars well into the future.

Retirement Obstacles to Prepare For

Those approaching retirement have a variety of potential retirement obstacles. Just a few of the additional concerns that retirees must address in his or her retirement planning include:

Outliving Assets and Income

With the vast increase in life expectancy over the last century, retirees are facing one of the biggest challenges in keeping retirement portfolios viable enough to last anywhere between twenty to forty years. Even though the improved medical technology of today is keeping people alive longer, there are many cases where those individuals are not necessarily living healthier. This can cause an additional strain on retirement portfolios in later years when additional health care costs must be deducted from limited assets or a finite stream of retirement income.

Potential Reductions in Social Security

In 1945, there were approximately thirty-five workers contributing to Social Security for every one retiree. For the last few decades, the number of retirees receiving Social Security has grown much faster than the tax-paying workforce. In fact, by 1995, there were only about three to four workers for every one retiree. Today the number is down to about two and nine tenths workers. With declining birth rates and increasing life expectancies, the Social Security system as we know it faces some serious challenges. It is expected that by the year 2036 there will only be two and one tenth workers contributing into the system for every one retiree receiving income benefits. In addition, by the year 2015, Social Security retirement benefit payments will begin to exceed the tax collections used to fund them.

Regardless of how, when, or if this government program is brought back to financial solvency, the truth is that Social Security was never meant to totally fund an individual's retirement income. In fact, this income stream was always meant to simply provide a supplement to other savings and retirement income sources. The Social Security System is still doable and can be made solvent with relative ease compared to many other challenges this nation is facing.

Potential Reductions in Medicare Coverage

It is reported that Medicare may actually be a five times larger deficit concern than Social Security! How's that for perspective?

With all of the new health care legislation recently passed, there are likely to be real cuts to programs that affect retirees and Medicare is no exception.

Estate Planning

There is a long-held misconception that a person must have a large estate in order to need an estate plan. Although the term estate plan may sound like it is only for the wealthy, the fact is that anyone with assets or loved ones to protect should seriously consider constructing a good solid estate plan. Without an estate plan in place, federal and state laws dictate how property, personal items, and assets will be divided without regard to the actual wishes of the individual.

Conflicts due to family issues and legal problems can often result tying up the estate, creating unfavorable tax consequences and slowing down the distribution of the assets. Oftentimes, these conflicts add excessive additional administrative, legal and tax-expense which must be deducted from the estate thereby reducing its overall value even before the distribution of assets to heirs.

All good intentions of leaving an inheritance for loved ones can come to a quick end if not properly planned out. When leaving an inheritance, one should never assume that things will be distributed the way that was intended unless there is a well-documented plan in place.

So, in order to avoid a big mess for loved ones that must be sorted out afterwards, time needs to be spent preparing. Experts recommend that one spend at least as much time (or more) working on inheritance issues as most would spend researching the purchase of a car or a home.

Maintaining Independence

Going hand-in-hand with the need for long-term care is the desire of retirees to maintain independence, especially if his or her health starts to decline. Oftentimes, an individual who needs assistance with basic daily living activities is able to remain at home; yet may need some assistance from home health care services. These types of services have significant costs and must be planned for accordingly.

Liquidity

All financial plans should include some degree of liquidity especially those of retirees. It is important to have cash available to cover any emergencies or other unexpected expenses that may come up. Liquid funds should not have just a negative correlation. Retirees may want to have some cash on hand that will allow for a nice vacation or to purchase that new car one has always wanted.

Spousal Impoverishment

A big concern for retirees who are married is that of preventing a spouse from facing impoverishment when one spouse predeceases the other. Certainly, there are many cases where upon the death of one spouse the survivor loses Social Security or pension income he or she had been counting on, not realizing that the way these plans originally were set up was to end or reduce income upon the death of one spouse. This can be extremely difficult financially for the surviving spouse and in some unfortunate circumstances can actually lead to impoverishment.

Obstacles in Summary

The aforementioned challenges and obstacles have contributed to today's new retirement paradigm shift—allowing MarketFree™ annuities to move to the forefront of being considered, recommended, and chosen on a widespread basis as a preferred asset class for the foundational portion of a well balanced portfolio.

Information of Interest

The Government Accountability Office (GAO) in July of 2011 issued a report that had the input of several credentialed financial analysts across the country. This report made it crystal clear that a majority of Americans are in trouble with retirements in general. The consensus was for most Americans who are in or near retirement to consider far more money placed in annuities and considerably less money in the stock market or other securities.

Ben Bernanke, Federal Reserve Chairman, on a personal level disclosed that the primary assets utilized for his own retirement consist of two annuities... hmmm. Since actions tend to speak louder than words, Mr. Bernanke just may have some insightful knowledge about the safety and benefits of annuities since he set up his own personal retirement with about one million dollars using these financial instruments!

Video: <u>What is Your Retirement Strategy...</u>

<u>Click to watch and consider your own retirement strategy...</u>

Video URL: <u>http://annuityguys.com/annuities-investing-and-retirement-whats-your-strategy</u>

QR Code for smart phones:

Chapter 2: All Advisors are the Same, NOT!

"Look, let's not dwell on the details Bill. Your retirement is in good hands. See! It is already paying dividends."

"Finance is the art of passing money from hand to hand until it finally disappears." - Robert W. Sarnoff

Case Study 1 -- Jill

Jill began sobbing quietly as she looked down at the table. *"I just don't understand how he could have done this to me,"* she said. *"He knew I was counting on this money for retirement. He knew that my savings were needed for me to take care of my mother as she gets older."* The magnitude of Jill's loss and feelings of betrayal showed in her eyes. Jill's quiet despair then turned into disgust and anger. *"Why would he do this?"* she repeated.

She had trusted her financial advisor of many years to protect her life savings. The nest egg Jill had relied on to get her through retirement had become a gambling chip for an advisor who clearly didn't have Jill's best interest at heart. She had insisted on safe and conservative investments as her retirement neared. However, without her full understanding or consent, her advisor had moderated her portfolio from a high-risk position to a lesser-risk position. Yet, her advisor had failed to remove Jill from the full-investment risk she had requested. Her life's savings were instead being used like gambling chips in a still-vulnerable market position. Nonetheless, Jill's advisor continued to reassure her that her portfolio was safe and secure.

Jill's complete trust in her longtime advisor would prove detrimental in the Great Recession of 2007-2009. In an instant, the security and comfort Jill had expected to have during her retirement years had quickly vanished.

Unfortunately, Jill's experience is all too common.

Financial Advisors with Divided Interests!

What Jill and so many others fail to understand is that financial advisors are not created equal. There are many different types of financial specialists, generalists, and self-serving salespeople masquerading as financial experts out there. Many times, the needs of the client and or investor are secondary to the interests of the advisor or companies the advisor represents.

In Jill's case, the financial advisor to whom she had trusted her entire life's savings actually was a registered representative working for a broker/dealer. Broker/dealers reward their representatives for selling specific investments by paying higher commissions. Sales quotas are common and representatives may be compelled to reach these quotas to preserve income levels or even to maintain continued employment.

While the representatives may portray themselves as honest and independent-thinking advisors, the reality is that his or her allegiance is divided between serving self-interests such as--commissions, the company represented, and the client's needs.

Registered representatives for this reason are not required to disclose everything known. There is no fiduciary responsibility to the client; the only requirement is to consider the suitability of the investment and be truthful about what is being sold rather than recommending what may actually be the best choice for the client.

Choosing an Advisor

With stories such as Jill's, selecting a financial advisor can be a bit intimidating. However, with a little preparedness and financial industry education, a person can approach this hurdle with a well founded confidence.

First, it is important to understand how financial advisors are paid because not all are compensated similarly. This knowledge can make a big difference in knowing if an advisor is financially motivated to work for the client's best interest and highest good.

Commission

There are certain financial advisors who are paid on a straight commission basis. This means that this type of advisor is paid a commission on each of the investment or insurance products they sell. The commissions they earn could be paid based on a variety of investment and insurance vehicles such as stocks, bonds, mutual funds, CDs, life insurance policies, and annuities they sell. As a general rule, all insurance products pay commissions to licensed advisors, producers and agents; the amount is paid by the insurance company and regulated by each states Department of Insurance.

Fee-Only

The fee-only pay structure helps to avoid the conflict of interest issue because the financial advisor is being paid a flat fee for financial planning services rendered. In this case, the advisor does not receive any sales or trading commissions on specific products that are recommended.

The irony of the "fee only" advisor's planning is that someone who makes a commission has to implement the fee only advisor's plan. This may create conflicts since the two may disagree for valid reasons, leaving the client confused after paying extra for fee-only advice.

Fee-Based

The fee-based compensation structure differs from that of the fee-only structure. With a fee-based system, the advisors' commissions --if any-- are in addition to the fee that is charged by the advisor. These commissions come from the investment or insurance products that the advisor recommends. Full disclosure is important with Fee-Based advisors so clients can weigh potential conflicts of interest.

Flat-Fee or Retainer

This structure allows for a preset fee that is determined and paid in advance, typically for financial planning needs. The advisor may still charge additional fees for various advisory services or receive commissions on certain financial products. Full disclosure is important with this fee structure so clients can weigh potential conflicts of interest.

Hourly Rate

Some financial advisors are paid a flat hourly rate for services rendered. This hourly rate is charged for the advisor's information and advice, similar to how lawyers charge for time. Advisors may or may not also be paid a commission which should be disclosed upfront.

Before a person begins a working relationship with a financial advisor, it is a good idea to work out in advance how the financial advisor will be paid. It is important to request a copy *in writing* of that compensation agreement before choosing to move forward. Full disclosure is important with this hourly fee structure so clients can weigh potential conflicts of interest.

Financial Advisor Titles & Descriptions

In addition to different types of pay structures, there are a variety of financial advisor descriptions. In other words, while many advisors may be able to offer the same or at least similar products, the advisors may have different titles or descriptions depending upon--what type of advisor they are--as well as indicating, his or her pay structure.

Titles and descriptions can also differ based on the various licensing that each advisor possesses as well as the types of products an advisor is allowed to sell.

Below are detailed descriptions of the types of financial advisors that may be encountered as one navigates the tributaries of choosing from the many types of financial professionals. These terms and descriptions will help with understanding each different advisor type, thus helping with the ability to choose a qualified and objective advisor rather than a company-loyal and commission-driven advisor, or one less qualified who may not serve individual needs and financial goals in an intelligent or objective way.

Keep in mind that no title makes anyone ethical or unethical it is possible for the least titled advisor to assist clients in the best possible way while the highest titled could use his or her position to deceive and harm clients. Start with understanding the title first, then do your comprehensive due-diligence--checking references, background checks, etc., and read this chapter for more due diligence suggestions.

Insurance Producer/Agent

Is an individual who sells insurance products; is licensed by the state or states in which the insurance is sold and receives commission.

Solicitor

Is a licensed individual who connects clients and third-party firms together for their mutual benefit, earning a fee or commission.

Stock Broker

An individual or a firm that is licensed to transact securities business earning a commission or what is commonly referred to as a load in addition to transaction fees based on selling securities for a brokerage firm.

Registered Representative

Is an individual who is technically employed by a broker/dealer and is considered an affiliated/employed representative, sharing loads, commissions, and other fees. Registered representatives are directly influenced by the directives of broker/dealer employers when it comes to investment choices and strategies that can be offered to clients.

Investment Advisor Representative

Is an individual who is supervised by a registered investment advisory firm as an affiliated advisor sharing financial planning-, and management-fees. Investment advisor representatives are directly influenced by the directives of his or her registered investment advisor supervisory firm when it comes to investment choices and strategies that can be offered to clients. This license requires the investment advisor to function as a fiduciary. Meaning, the advisor is to act for the highest good to benefit the client while providing full disclosure.

Registered Investment Advisor

This is a firm (not an individual) licensed by the State Department of Securities or the SEC to give investment advice via investment advisor representatives who also can manage investments on a fee basis with full disclosure. This license requires an investment advisor to function as a fiduciary. Meaning, the investment advisor is to act for the highest good to benefit the client while providing full disclosure.

Independent Agent/Investment Advisor Representative and a Principal of a Registered Investment Advisory Firm

This is a description of an individual combining a few of the above titles who is dual licensed, independent, and able to represent any company that might be of benefit to clients. An independent investment advisor representative - who is also the principal of his or her Registered Investment Advisory Firm - is an individual licensed by the SEC or the State Department of Securities to give investment advice and manage investments on a fee basis with full disclosure. When investment advisor representatives are independent and also act as the principal of a firm, a full range of investment services can be offered to clients with no outside supervisory directives interfering with what may be best for the client.

These investment advisors are licensed to function as a fiduciary, which requires the investment advisor to act for the highest good to benefit the client while providing full disclosure. This type of investment advisor would also be insurance licensed. State law regulates agents and has oversight of insurance compensation paid by insurance companies to licensed agents or advisors.

In summation, *fiduciary-responsibility* - possessing the highest legal level of responsibility beneficial to the interest of the client, is the most important aspect to consider in all of the above mentioned financial titles. This is also known as the Prudent Man rule: assisting clients in the same manner as the advisor or agent would assist a close friend, family member, or as the advisor would choose services or products for his or her own benefit.

Professional Designations

In addition to titles and required licenses, financial advisors can obtain additional professional industry designations. These designations are not required for an advisor to offer certain products or services. However, these do indicate that advisors are serious about the work that they do and want to attain additional knowledge and credentials in their chosen field. Some of these professional industry designations include:

CFP® - Certified Financial Planner

In order to earn the CFP designation, advisors must pass extensive exams in the areas of financial planning, taxes, insurance, estate planning, and retirement. And to maintain this designation, regular annual continuing education courses are required.

CRPC® - Chartered Retirement Planning Counselor

Individuals who hold the CRPC® designation have completed a course of study encompassing pre-and post-retirement needs, asset management, estate planning and the entire retirement planning process using models and techniques from real client situations. Additionally, individuals must pass an end-of-course examination that tests their ability to synthesize complex concepts and apply theoretical concepts to real-life situations. (http://cffpdesignations.com/Designation/CRPC)

ChFC® - Chartered Financial Consultant

To earn this designation, an advisor must meet requirements –training and experience, as well as passing exams covering finance and investing. Experience requirements include having at least three years of active involvement in the financial industry. The course covers topics in financial planning, income taxation, insurance, investments, and estate planning.

CLU® - Chartered Life Underwriter

This designation is granted to advisors who complete an intensive training in the areas of life insurance and personal financial planning. Course topics include insurance, investments, taxation, employee benefits, estate planning, accounting, management, and economics.

RHU® - Registered Health Underwriter

Those who are RHUs have completed educational requirements in the area of health insurance. They are trained in offering clients the best products as well as ethical advice.

REBC® - Registered Employee Benefits Consultant

REBCs are extensively trained to provide the most knowledgeable, current, and ethical advice possible regarding group benefit plans for companies. They are also schooled on retirement needs for business owners and employees.

CSA - Certified Senior Advisor

This designation indicates advisors who have accepted a code of ethics for working with older individuals in addition to equipping themselves with important knowledge and practical tools significant to better understand and serve older clients at the highest level. *This is not a financial designation.*

CLTC - Certified in Long-Term Care

This designation indicates an advisor's specialized training to work in the field of long-term care planning. It also helps provide legal, accounting, insurance, and financial service professionals the tools necessary to address this type of subject matter with an age appropriate individual.

It's Time to Decide on an Advisor!

Having a rudimentary understanding of the framework in which many of these financial advisors work will go a long way in helping to select a professional whose job is to secure a future retirement. Choosing a superior advisor will mean examining many aspects of the prospective advisor's professional and personal life.

Ideally, the financial professional being considered must have written extensively about his or her advisory perspective, financial services, and experience. This written information should be readily available in the public arena such as websites, books, newsletters, columns, or other venues to which the financial professional routinely contributes. Advisors strategies, philosophies, and retirement planning approach should be a clear indication of how effective he or she will be at meeting a future retiree's financial goals; that advisors position should be clear, informative, and aligning with the values of the individual considering the advisor.

Also, pertinent to selecting the appropriate advisor is determining the degree to which the advisor is truly independent. An independent advisor will typically have more access to an extensive array of planning options. This type of advisor will be in a better position to choose the best solution based on the needs of the client. Independent advisors are not subject to the limited choices and required quotas which the vast majority of other advisors are limited by.

How Financial Advisors Are Regulated

Individuals and entities that engage in providing investment advice to others are regulated by federal or state regulators and sometimes both. In fact, before being allowed to offer any financial advice, sell and etc., financial advisors are typically required to be educated (pre-licensure requirements fulfilled) in specific areas of expertise, pass certain licensure exams, complete required continuing education as well as anti-money laundering required exams – of which exams and courses required are dependent upon the type of advice or financial products that will be provided by the licensed advisor.

Most advisors, especially those who are involved in offering securities are required to take and pass a standardized national securities examination. And while registration varies from state to state, investment advisors are required in each state to register with the state or the federal Securities Exchange Commission (SEC) when licensed; pay a fee for processing the application; disclose certain information to the securities agency or the public, or both; and maintain a bond or a minimum amount of net capital.

Financial advisors are also required to keep certain records. For example, all advisors must maintain past marketing and advertising materials, receipts and disbursement journals, a general ledger, bank records, records of bills and statements, and all financial statements for specific number of years. In addition, they must also maintain records of all written communications and agreements including electronic transmissions; keep a client database of - information, forms and suitability records.

Some good news is that the regulatory agencies make it simple to check the background of a financial advisor. For example: the Financial Industry Regulatory Authority (FINRA) maintains an online database that holds licensing and registration information on over 650,000 active registered advisors nationwide at this website: http://www.finra.org/brokercheck. This database allows people to find out about an advisor's employment history over the last ten years, the status of licensing and registration, and any disciplinary history. Before working with an advisor, it is a good idea to do a check out this website first. Then, one can feel much more certain about a financial advisor's background before trusting the advisor with one's retirement savings.

Questions to Ask a Prospective Advisor

- Is the prospective financial advisor properly licensed and experienced enough to recommend financial services in a manner that serves the client's best interest?

- Does the advisor have time-tested, real-life experience having gone through recessions, downturns, stagflation, and many other economic difficulties?

- Has the advisor had investment experience with his or her own personal finances?

- Is the advisor a generalist or a practicing specialist experienced in the disciplines that are pertinent to the client's stated needs?

- Does the advisor have a specialized, broad, or a general education background?

- Has the advisor assembled a portfolio of readily available validation documents (license, E&O insurance, specialized education, associations, awards, authored educational material, credentials, and etc.) including verifiable references?

- Is there a detailed advisor agreement of the services that are provided including fees or charges?

- Has the advisor written and published any publicly distributed financial books, editorials, or commentaries indicative of professional expertise? Is he or she a regional or nationally recognized contributor of financial knowledge to various publications?

- Does the advisor openly comply with stated codes of professional ethics? Is the advisor able to pass a personal and professional background check?

- Does the advisor belong to as a member (in good quality standing) the local Chamber of Commerce or other civic organizations?

- Does the advisor have affiliations with professional societies or associations?

- What is the advisor's track record concerning client retention?

These are tough yet fair questions that should be addressed before an individual investor or retiree determines the best financial advisor who could certainly help with his or her financial future.

In consonance to the above questions, there are many other observations every individual should make when considering a prospective financial advisor such as:

Considering how the prospective advisor introduced himself. This may seem a trivial matter; however, a financial person who solicits business by cold calling or a similar method probably is in need of business and may not be as experienced or has not achieved a higher level of success that is preferred by most clients.

Similarly, if an advisor has offered to meet at one's home to discuss financial concerns, it is possible this advisor has too much time on his or her hands. One should ask *why*. An effective financial planner is typically in high demand with very little time to visit client's homes. On the contrary, if having a scheduled appointment with the potential financial advisor at his or her office, take this opportunity to observe the office dynamics. Is the office tidy and uncluttered? Is the office environment busy and efficient?

However insignificant one might find these characteristics personally, these observations can be indicative of how effective the potential advisor will be for clients. An advisor worth consideration should be organized and in demand. There are exceptions to many of these types of observations, however, being aware and weighing many of these factors helps with making a favorable decision.

Any financial advisor regardless of license, title, and education may be objective and fair or selfishly biased, ethics and regard for a client's financial well-being must first come from any advisors moral compass. It may help to have an advisor with a legal fiduciary obligation who must unselfishly look out for client's best interest and not what pays more to the advisor. A financial planner who begins the initial meeting with suggestions to purchase stocks, annuities, or mutual funds without in-depth knowledge of an individual's financial situation should cause one to quickly gather belongings and leave the building! This advisor cannot possibly know what investments or insurance products will be in the best interests of an individual without first understanding the person's present financial situation.

Just as no one should ever take medications for an undiagnosed disease, one should never take advice from a financial planner who has not given one's portfolio a "thorough physical" in the light of the client's stated financial objectives.

Subjects an Advisor Should Ask About

- Retirement goals and objectives;
- Beginning of retirement Age;
- Present income;
- Monthly gross income need be at an expected retirement age, including all expenses and taxes;
- Marital status; number of children and grandchildren, if any;
- Home ownership;
- Present debts and cash outflows;
- Possible large one-time expenses in the future;
- Hobbies, collections, and things enjoyed in life;
- Present health;
- Age of parents living, if any;
- Estate plan, a will or a trust – if any;
- Importance of money to an individual retiree and or investor in terms of retirement income and leaving to heirs;
- Worries about money, if any;
- Couple of things an individual retiree and or investor's could change about his or her financial situation, if given the chance.

These are just *some* of the questions a qualified advisor will ask! An advisor who is not asking these questions cannot appreciate an individual's financial needs, and is therefore not qualified to manage investments or give financial advice on any person's behalf.

The Client's Responsibilities

Indeed, while it is true that finding an advisor with favorable professional traits is critical to one's financial well-being, it is on the other hand equally important that a client commits and contributes to the relationship, as well.

Upon selecting an advisor, it's crucially important that clients are comfortable with the financial service provider or investment advisor chosen. For this reason, one must be willing to disclose any and all information that could potentially affect the retirement decisions the client and advisor should make together.

Once an advisor is selected, determine beforehand how the advisor wishes to be compensated and ask for a written agreement that spells out the services that will be provided and the fees that will be charged. Financial advisors should always disclose commission arrangements from investment or insurance options recommended. Compensation should be clearly stated. An advisor who is paid based on *what product* is chosen has an inherent conflict of interest that should be disclosed and discussed. This discussion should define clear expectations and help avoid the possibility of self serving advisor interests.

It is the client's responsibility to ensure that the advisor clearly understands the financial objectives and the degree of risk one is comfortable with. The best of advisors will find it impossible to design a successful retirement plan without the proper client cooperation and information with which to work.

What's more, if the client has questions or concerns or if a particular matter is unclear, it is up to the client to ask the advisor for clarity. If a client does not voice any concern, the financial advisor is likely to assume the client is in agreement and understands. Silence could be misconstrued as complicity and prove unfavorable for one's financial well-being, by manifesting unsatisfactory future consequences.

On the same note, a superior financial advisor will exercise patience when explaining unfamiliar matters. After all, it is the client's portfolio and financial future hanging in the balance. The client should understand all the basic aspects of the full retirement plan.

No matter how distinguished or experienced the financial advisor selected may be; a client's financial well-being ultimately rests in his or her own hands. If one intends to secure assets for future retirement, there is no room for complacency in this process.

Clients must be diligent and do his or her homework. Know the advisor and monitor the portfolio carefully and frequently. In the end, the choices one makes or procrastinates on will help to either secure or destabilize twenty or more years of retirement.

The value of working closely together with an objective financial expert or a team of objective experts cannot be overemphasized.

Video: <u>Avoiding a Bad Advisor Experience</u>

<u>Click & Find out by watching this video...</u>

Video URL: <u>http://annuityguys.com/avoid-annuity-gimmicks-amateurs-and-charlatans</u>

Video QR Code for smart phones:

Chapter 3: Annuities -- Not Created Equal!

"Let's see, this annuity has the 50/50 guarantee. If we tear up the contract, we get both pieces??? What the x*-%-#?"

"Money is better than poverty, if only for financial reasons."
- Woody Allen

Case Study 2 -- Jane

Jane was contemplating making some changes to her investments based on recently retiring from her long-term employer. She was seventy years old and had been advised by her son, John, to consider an annuity that would provide her with some type of income stream in addition to her pension and Social Security retirement benefits.

Jane had $250,000 to invest and she wanted an income stream to begin immediately. In researching annuities, however, Jane and her son realized that there were many different types of annuities available and were having a difficult time deciding upon what would be the best choice for her.

After it was explained, Jane realized that with some annuities, she can have choices as to how interest was earned based on how her annuity's account value was allocated; and that income payouts were based not only on factors such as gender and life expectancy but also on her choices as to how and when income is received.

Based on Jane's age and gender, her life expectancy at that time was an additional seventeen years. With her allocation of $250,000, Jane could receive differing amounts of monthly income, depending upon the amount of time she chose to receive it.

For example, should Jane decide on a life immediate annuity with a ten year period certain, based on then-current interest rates in a fixed immediate annuity, Jane would receive a monthly income stream of $2,575. The ten year period certain allows the income stream to be redirected to John as Jane's son and beneficiary in the event of her pre-mature death. John would receive whatever is left of the income not yet paid out over the ten year period of certain income promised contractually.

However, with all other factors being equal, should Jane decide to opt for a life immediate annuity with no period certain where her income stream is also guaranteed throughout the remainder of her life, then Jane's monthly income amount would be $2,660.

Should Jane decide to place her funds into a fixed, hybrid, or variable annuity using an income rider or annuitization, her monthly income amount would be different still, and a variable annuity's lifetime guaranteed income could also fluctuate based on the performance of the underlying investments.

It is not always easy, with so many choices available, when deciding which type of annuity is best. When considering an annuity, it is essential to go into the decision with clear financial goals as to what the annuity is supposed to accomplish.

Understanding Annuities

Annuities can be funded in a couple of different ways. For example, the holder of an annuity may choose to fund it with periodic or systematic payments or with one lump sum payment. And there is a wide variety of annuity types to choose from, each with its own special features and benefits as well as pros and cons as to why they would or would not suit the specific goals of an individual.

For example, MarketFree™ fixed annuities pay a set amount of interest every year, while variable annuities earn a fluctuating or variable return based on the performance of the underlying investments. There are also several variations of MarketFree™ annuities that combine some characteristics of fixed, immediate and variable annuities, these are often referred to as hybrid annuities.

Certainly, one of the most popular reasons that people use annuities is to provide income in retirement. In fact, annuities may be referred to as "financial instruments" that offer an income that cannot be outlived (although this can be an incorrect stereotype depending upon the type of annuity or optional income payout that is chosen).

Annuities can be annuitized or an optional income rider can be activated to contractually guarantee a lifetime of guaranteed income; and there are different options on the timing of an annuity income stream as well. For example, if an individual chooses an immediate annuity that means that the annuity will begin to produce income soon after funding the annuity with a lump sum. Deferred annuities, on the other hand, are growing over time which means that the income withdrawal time frame will be deferred until a date in the future.

The deferral aspect of annuities, over time, allows their cash value to increase--including their guaranteed future income--which can be determined independently of their cash value account in some annuities. And after the deferral period, the annuity can predictably produce more contractually guaranteed retirement income for the holder of that annuity. All deferred annuities enjoy tax deferral with no income tax requirement until withdrawal. Re-investing money that would otherwise be paid out in tax over an extended period of years is always an advantage. This is a definite advantage over many investments like CDs, mutual funds, and dividend paying securities-oriented investments for a long-term retirement plan. Moreover, deferred annuities have several other benefits, yet to be explained in detail, that are significant for retirement planning.

A long-term MarketFree™ fixed annuity with an index option can potentially outperform CDs, bonds, and treasuries--they also have over specific five and ten year time periods outperformed many popular stock indices. Fixed annuities are not specifically designed to outperform the stock market even though it has been documented in the past.

So, are annuities good or bad? In and of themselves, annuities--just like any other investment--are not technically good or bad. An annuity can, however, be considered appropriate or inappropriate for one's particular situation. And while annuities can be used in a variety of situations, they are not necessarily the right choice for everyone. For example, deferred annuities are generally not as appropriate for younger individuals who have not yet maximized contributions to 401(k)s or other qualified plans, or do not have a long-term retirement objective as a goal.

In any case, when an individual funds an annuity contract issued by an insurance company, the annuity owner can feel secure knowing that a safe financial instrument has been chosen which can grow to enhance wealth and provide an income for life in addition to other retirement benefits and guarantees not available with traditional market related investments.

Different Types of Annuities

Annuities come in many shapes and sizes and offer many choices.

However, some of names and descriptions are simply redundancy in terminology. There are many terms that actually refer to the same type or benefit of an annuity and it is easy to become quite confused. Annuities are classified or named based on--risk, safety, premium payments, accumulation, death benefits and income or withdrawal provisions such as:

Immediate Annuity is a type of MarketFree™ annuity where one single lump sum premium payment is made. The lump sum or cash asset is forfeited permanently in exchange for a guaranteed income. Typically, income payments from this type of annuity will begin right away but no later than twelve months from purchase. Immediate annuities are normally obtained when an individual needs steady income during or prior to retirement. Immediate annuities may be either fixed or variable. If the immediate annuity is variable, then the amount of the income payments may change over time depending upon the performance of the underlying investments.

SPIA (Single Premium Immediate Annuity) annuities are funded with a single lump sum premium payment and then they typically will begin within thirty days to one year making regular monthly income payments to the annuitant (Same as an Immediate Annuity).

Lifetime Annuities offer a way for an individual to receive a guaranteed income for life regardless of how long that is. The income payments from the annuity will begin at a specific time and the amount of payment is calculated based on the annuitant's life span (calculated by insurance company actuaries). Lifetime annuities literally offer an income stream that the annuitant cannot outlive. Typically these are considered immediate annuities but may also refer to a deferred annuity offering annuitization or a lifetime income rider option.

A **Period Certain Immediate Annuity** is an annuity that will guarantee income payments for life. If the annuitant is to pass away during that period of time, the income will continue to be paid out to his or her beneficiary until the period certain or period of years guaranteed by the annuity has ended. Therefore, if the annuity holder had selected a fifteen-year period certain and passes away after the eighth year, then his or her beneficiary would receive income from that annuity for an additional seven years. If the annuitant remains living, income is received for as many years as needed even after the period certain benefit for heirs has ended. (Same as an Immediate Annuity with a death benefit option)

Certain Period Annuity is an annuity that will guarantee income payments for a specific period of time and *not for life*. Typically, the income is paid out to the annuitant until the specified time period ends. If the annuitant is to pass away during that period of time, the income will continue to be paid out to his or her beneficiary until the time period on the annuity has ended. (Same as an Immediate Annuity with a death benefit option, but, based on a limited payment period)

An **Income Annuity** can either be a fixed or a variable annuity that pays the annuity holder an amount of money on an annual or monthly basis. Typically, the payments will begin within thirty days after the person funds the annuity. The length of time that payments are made can be based either on the lifetime of the annuitant or the lifetime of the annuitant's spouse. (The same as an immediate annuity)

There is also a **Pension Annuity.** When an individual retires from a company, the retiree may have a choice of receiving either a pension annuity or a lump sum of cash from the pension plan. The pension annuity can be voluntarily contracted by the individual and it offers a stream of regular payments that are received by that former employee for life or for a specified period. This is a form of an immediate annuity.

MarketFree™ Fixed Annuities are a type of financial instrument offered by insurance companies that defer income benefits guaranteeing principal/premium and interest over the life of the annuity contract. In this case, *the insurance company takes on all investment risk insulating and protecting the annuity owner*. There are many versions of fixed annuities.

SPDA (Single Premium Deferred Annuity) deferred annuities are funded with one lump sum premium payment. The annuitant will not receive income payments or the account value until a time in the future. These annuities - fixed or variable have two separate phases. First, the savings or accumulation phase where funds in the account can grow. Second is the income phase where the annuitant receives income from the annuity.

And with a **Single Premium Fixed Deferred Annuity,** in the income phase--payments will be fixed, increasing, or fluctuating as contractually specified and lifetime payouts are also guaranteed by the claims paying ability of the insurance company.

A **Flexible Premium Fixed Deferred Annuity** has the flexibility to be funded with varying premium payments or lump sums. These premium payments may be made systematically or at different times and in differing amounts (typically with a set minimum amount per premium payment). The income benefits will begin at a time in the future and these payments will be a fixed or increasing. Income benefits to the annuitant are clearly defined and thus contractually guaranteed by the insurance company.

A **MYGA (Multi Year Guaranteed Annuity)** or **CD Type Annuity** offers similarities that are close to a certificate of deposit (CD). These fixed annuities guarantee a fixed rate of return throughout the entire duration of the annuities contractual maturity or surrender charge period--typically anywhere between one and ten years. Rates will vary depending upon the issuing insurance company. While both are considered safe, only CDs have FDIC insurance which has the full backing of the U.S government

Another annuity is a **Guaranteed Interest Contract--Annuity (GIC)**. This fixed annuity offers a guaranteed minimum interest rate that will be credited by the insurance company throughout the accumulation period of the annuity contract, similar to certificates of deposit issued by banks.

One may also choose a **MarketFree™ Index Annuity**. This fixed annuity has an extra option for higher potential interest rates being linked to a market indicator such as a popular stock market index that provides an objective benchmark for determining interest earned. This type of fixed annuity coupled with an income rider is also considered "*a hybrid mixture of a fixed, variable, and an immediate annuity.*" principal that is allocated to an index annuity is protected from any downside investment risk. If there are gains, a portion of the gains from the index performance will be added to the index annuity as interest. Meanwhile, a **Fixed Index Deferred Annuity** is an index annuity wherein during the growth stage, the income benefit payments do not begin until a time decided upon in the future.

Several names for a MarketFree™ Fixed Annuity with the option to earn interest by linking to an external index are:

Index Annuity, Indexed Annuity, Fixed Index Annuity, Fixed

Indexed Annuity, Equity Indexed Annuity, Equity Index Annuity, Ratchet Annuity, Ratchet Index Annuity, Hybrid Annuity, Hybrid Index Annuity or Hybrid Income Annuity.

The most accurate and correct name is simply a Fixed Annuity with an index option.

Again, the income payments on an index annuity can either be immediate or deferred. This annuity differs from other types of fixed annuities due to the way interest is earned. They have an additional option that credits interest based on linking a popular market index to the annuities account value, while having no downside market risk. All fixed index annuities have a minimum guarantee of interest or return of principal that is calculated at a rate that is established in the annuity contract, and also offer a current fixed interest rate option in lieu of the index option that is declared by the insurer from year to year. Moreover, a **Fixed Index Deferred Annuity** is considered a fixed annuity in the accumulation stage that has not been annuitized.

Ratchet Annuity. This term is again used in reference to the fixed index annuity. It refers to every year or specified time period the account values in the annuity are locked in and the index is reset to "ratchet upward" in order to include the gain for that particular year as locked in principal. Therefore, the principal that is in the annuity account is adjusted upward and will essentially form the new base of guaranteed principal upon which the future upward index calculations are made. In this case, the account value will never be adjusted downward which assures annuity holders that there will be no loss of any principal or interest earnings as the annuity ratchets upwards.

Variable Annuity, in its most basic sense defers income and allows the annuity holder to allocate the premium dollars into different types of investments or subaccounts. The value of these investments will fluctuate based on market conditions and performance of those underlying investments. However, there are several forms that variable annuities can take.

The **Tax Sheltered Annuity** allows employees of public education or other tax-exempt organizations to make pretax contributions through salary reduction into a tax-sheltered retirement plan. The employees are thus not taxed on the amount of the contribution until making withdrawals later in retirement. This term applies, for example, to a 403(b) plan variable annuity.

A **Single Premium Variable Deferred Annuity** is funded with one lump sum premium payment. Income payments to the annuity holder may begin immediately or at some time in the future depending upon whether the annuity is immediate or deferred. The income benefits to the annuitant can vary based upon market conditions and the underlying investments chosen.

With a **Flexible Premium Variable Deferred Annuity**, the frequency of the premium payment can vary and the amount of the premium may also vary (subject to a minimum amount). The income benefits to the annuitant can vary based upon market conditions and the underlying investments chosen. The underlying investments in the contract are tied to market risks and rewards, thus can fluctuate widely in value having a substantial positive or negative effect on income.

A **Living Benefit Variable Annuity** can offer benefits during retirement provided certain conditions are met, such as the annuity holder having lifetime income rider allowing majority control of his or her asset or a catastrophic/terminal illness rider with no surrender fees or penalties. Different insurance companies have different rules with regard to the amount of money that may be withdrawn from the annuity when receiving the benefits early.

Individual Retirement Annuity is an annuity equivalent to an IRA (individual retirement account). However, in the case of the annuity just like a traditional investment or bank issued IRA, the annuity contract needs to be issued in the name of the annuity owner; even though the annuity owner's spouse, under certain conditions, may be allowed to receive survivor benefits from this annuity.

For those interested in leaving money to a charity, there is the **Gift Annuity**. This annuity provides an arrangement in which a charitable organization pays out income to an annuitant (and possibly also the annuitant's spouse) in return for an irrevocable transfer of property or cash.

There are even annuities that may be purchased by members of various organizations such as a **Fraternal Annuity.** It is an annuity that is offered to members of a fraternal organization like the Knights of Columbus or any other group that is not formed for the sole purpose of participating in insurance or investments with their members. Fraternal annuities are not protected by FDIC or the State Insurance Guarantee Association (SIGA).

There are many different types of annuities to learn about. This is a fairly comprehensive list but it is not exhaustive. After becoming acquainted with the various qualities and redundancies of these financial instruments, it is essential to have a financial expert further clarify the inner workings of each one to help narrow one's search as to what is possibly the most beneficial annuity for a retiree's unique situation.

Choosing an Annuity

An annuity is defined as a sum of money that is paid to an annuity owner in intervals for a specified amount of time, often perpetually for life in return for premium paid with installments or in a single payment. The annuities outlined above for--retirement income, savings growth, and investment are made available primarily by insurance companies and some fraternal organizations.

Annuities; MarketFree™ fixed or variable, are tax-deferred (except for immediate annuities that begin income right away or within twelve months) which means that the earnings from interest with fixed annuities or growth from investments inside of a variable annuity are tax-deferred until interest or earnings are withdrawn. Holders of an annuity are only taxed when taking the systematic income distributions or if owners randomly withdraw funds from the account. In addition, the earnings in most scenarios may not be withdrawn without an IRS imposed tax penalty until the annuity owner reaches age fifty-nine and a half, except in very specific circumstances.

Annuities can be separated into two primary categories. These categories are established based on the risk characteristics of each type of primary annuity; variable or fixed. Each of the two categories of annuities, with their variations and options, serves a particular purpose.

A fixed annuity will guarantee a minimum amount including all principal plus interest back to the owner with **the insurer accepting any and**

all investment risk.

On the contrary, variable annuity does not offer such a guarantee. **The owner accepts all of the investment risk;** however, one does have the potential for a higher return depending on the performance of the underlying investments.

Within these two categories, annuities are further separated into income variants known as immediate and deferred. These terms indicate when modal income may begin.

In order to determine the type of annuity that will best serve individual financial objectives, it is important to look at one's age, size of assets, future income needs, and inflation projections. And taken with a cash-flow analysis over one's life expectancy, these factors should narrow the field and point to the type of annuity or investment that best suits most retirees.

Some annuities may be significantly better than others when it comes to planning for retirement. For example, a MarketFree™ fixed annuity would not likely be a good choice for someone who is under the age of thirty-five. This is because individuals in this age category should be more focused on growing assets rather than avoiding investment risk or receiving an income from savings or investments at this stage in life. An exception could be based on disability or extreme aversion to risk.

Retirees on the other hand, need to place more of a focus on protecting assets with little or no investment risk and to contractually guarantee an income stream during retirement. In this case, a MarketFree™ annuity can provide a recognized relatively safe option to accomplish this objective. And if combined with other portfolio investments, annuities can be a foundational portfolio asset allocation for nearly anyone approaching retirement or who is currently retired. It would be expected that individuals with a number of years left until retirement would likely opt for deferred annuities for future income needs, while some retirees may need an immediate annuity or a deferred annuity with the popular new income riders to supplement his or her present income.

Age can be a strong influence on the degree of risk an investor is willing to take. People with several years until retirement might feel that it is probable to recover any losses that might occur with a less-conservative annuity or a securities investment. Yet retirement-aged individuals might select a more cautious approach. Investors who may have gotten a late start in saving for retirement might also choose riskier investments with the hopes of making up for lost time. This may not be a well thought-out strategy. It is more akin to gambling or going for broke!

For those who are worried about income keeping up with inflation and a cost of living adjustment (COLA) during retirement, a rider can be added to some annuities which address this inflation concern. Yes, there is typically a rider cost for this annuity income benefit each year to help the individual's income keep up with the rising cost of living.

Choosing the appropriate annuity can be a tricky undertaking. If one does not have an advisor to help navigate the complexities of retirement planning, this might be a good time to consider turning to a knowledgeable professional with experience in structuring annuities for an optimized portfolio. Making a mistake at this level of planning can be a very expensive lesson or cause irreversible damage to say the least.

Video: <u>What is The Best Annuity?</u>

<u>Click & Watch this video to find out...</u>

Video URL: http://annuityguys.com/the-best-annuity

QR code for smart phones:

Chapter 4: MarketFree™ Fixed Annuities

"Since I retired, my wife is forcing me to live healthy and stay out of HER SPACE! Is it possible to UN-RETIRE?"

"Good judgment is usually the result of experience, and experience frequently is the result of bad judgment." -Robert Lovell

Case Study 3 -- Jan and Steve

In November of 2007, Jan and Steve, a couple concerned about the security of their investments and retirement savings made a call to Ed, a family friend who was also their financial advisor. After a brief conversation they agreed to meet a few days later to discuss their portfolio.

Upon meeting with the couple, Ed reluctantly agreed with the couple; that they were not risk-takers and yet he had a majority of their assets wrapped up in the stock market against their better judgment. Awkward as it was, Jan and Steve severed their business relationship with Ed causing some friction among the relatives.

In an initial consultation with a new advisor, Jan and Steve were carefully examining their investment options and looking at alternatives such as CDs, bonds, and REITs. The couple also discussed that they had read some negative reviews about annuities. The sources they were quoting said that annuities were risky and associated with high fees and high surrender charges. The articles they had gathered their information from were strongly biased with negative stereotypes. These articles had placed all emphasis on the variable annuity (VA) category as if all annuities were cut from the same cloth which was careless and unfair. Unfortunately, it is not at all uncommon for financial writers to demonstrate bias by spinning an incomplete or simply inaccurate portrayal of annuities. Although the VA, when used under correct circumstances, can make perfect sense. They are distinctly different from fixed annuities which are no- or low-fee, low- or no-risk and far more conservative for retirement planning purposes.

Once they understood the differences between variable and fixed, the couple wanted to learn more about the benefits of using a fixed annuity for a portion of their retirement portfolio.

This couple eventually chose to leave the stock market and allocated a sizeable portion of their retirement savings into fixed annuities with income riders. Their cash value has increased as planned and they are now comfortable knowing their retirement income foundation is predictable and secure. Best of all, they did not lose any of their money during the Great Recession of 2007-2009.

Unfortunately, not all misinformed individuals have such a happy ending.

The History of Fixed Annuities

In 1759, the first annuity was offered in the United States from a company in Pennsylvania to Presbyterian ministers and their families. This company eventually evolved into the Pennsylvania Company for Insurance on Lives and Granting Annuities and in 1912, it began offering annuities to the general public. Typically, these were fixed annuities that offered some type of guarantee to the annuitant.

Several years later in the 1930s, annuities became more popular due to concerns about the financial markets in the U.S. following the Great Depression. (Hmm, sounds familiar!) And, it was around this same time that New Deal programs were encouraging individuals to save for retirement. To help with this, many corporate pension plans were also created.

In 1995, a new type of fixed annuity was introduced which had an option for linking to a market index to enhance higher interest growth having a ratchet feature--locked in--account value and death benefit along with it. Index annuities are based on linked market index performance, typically a popular market or commodity index provides the basis for determining interest earnings to be applied at a specified point in time and then locked in having no downside risk. The ratchet feature allows an annuity's gains to be locked in and used as a starting point or base for the annuity's new account value.

That same year in 1995, sales of all annuities topped the $100 billion mark indicating that these products were being used by many in the accumulation of retirement assets and it only took about five more years before total annuity assets in the United States topped the $1 trillion mark.

In recent years, many additional features were added to annuities including the guaranteed minimum withdrawal benefit, the guaranteed minimum accumulation benefit, and the guaranteed lifetime withdrawal benefit.

Recent tax law changes have allowed annuities to include a tax free withdrawal on a long-term care rider.

By 2007, total annuity assets in the United States had climbed to nearly $2 trillion. And by the end of 2010, variable annuities alone accounted for $1.5 trillion in assets. That, coupled with fixed annuity assets has brought the total amount of annuity assets to well over $2.2 trillion.

The future of annuities is looking even brighter as insurance companies come out with more innovations to accommodate the seventy-eight million retiring baby boomers. Insurance companies are designing annuities that are more beneficial and retirement friendly to fit the needs of this new generation of retirees.

Fact or Fiction - Know the Truth!

Fact or Fiction: Many investments offer a guaranteed income stream. — Fiction!

With the exception of pension plans and Social Security, annuities are the only financial planning option that will guarantee a continuous stream of income throughout the duration of one's life.

Since the average life span of most Americans has increased significantly throughout the last few decades, many retirees now face an increased possibility of outliving savings and investments. Sensibly, many retirees have included annuities into portfolios as a means of having foundational income guarantees to hedge against inflation and to defer paying tax as the annuity portion of the portfolio grows for future income or wealth accumulation.

Annuities can provide added assurance that comfort and security will continue on long after retirees have left the workplace. Annuities also have the added benefit of providing retirees with a means to begin or increase retirement income.

Fact or Fiction: MarketFree™ Fixed annuities are risky investments that can lose principal. — Fiction!

Individuals who held MarketFree™ fixed annuities prior to 2007 were a little concerned that they may have played it *too* safe with the portfolio. Fixed annuities held the unrepentant reputation of being modest in growth, secure, and unexciting.

Needless to say - after millions of people lost substantial net wealth during the 2008-2009 Great Recession, MarketFree™ fixed annuity owners were quite satisfied that they had made a wise choice by securing their future net worth. The safety net surrounding the fixed annuity had proven invaluable to many who opted for this boring, yet predictable, "tried and true" retirement allocation.

Fact or Fiction: Fixed annuities earn about the same as banks and never earn what stocks do over any considerable time span. — Fiction!

Both fixed annuities and CDs are often considered the prudent means in which to guarantee principal and assist in a secure financial future. Indeed, both of these options are good candidates for the risk-wary investor or for the foundational safety allocations in a risk-oriented portfolio.

However, when compared, fixed annuities typically offer interests rates 1 to 3 percent higher than that of CDs. In fact, from 1999 to 2009, fixed annuities have actually outperformed many stock index market returns and could potentially continue to do so over the next decade or two as volatility giveth and taketh away.

Fact or Fiction: Annuities have a 10 percent IRS penalty for early withdrawals on earnings before age fifty-nine and a half. — Fact!

Fixed annuities and CDs are both subject to issuer surrender fees upon early withdrawal. However, individual owners who are likely to need funds prior to retirement age may opt for CDs, money-market, or securities-oriented investments in order to avoid the additional 10 percent IRS tax penalty, on individuals under fifty-nine and one half years of age, levied against early withdrawals' *on earnings only* from deferred annuities.

Fact or Fiction: Annuities have penalty-free withdrawals each year until the maturity of the contract. — Fact!

No matter how we might attempt to prepare for a future full of unpredictable circumstance, life will inevitably throw the occasional curveball. Unlike many investment options, annuities have a built-in cushion for just such instances.

Most annuities offer up to an annual 10 percent withdrawal of the principal and interest the annuity has gained without penalty which reduces the risk in situations when liquid funds are needed unexpectedly. Also, many annuities contain waivers included in the contract to remove surrender charges in the case of serious illness or other such unforeseen circumstances. This is not the case with other investment options such as mutual funds, CDs, or bonds.

Annuity surrender charges have been at times overstated by naysayers to discourage retirees from making annuity allocations that can be genuinely beneficial in the long run.

Fact or Fiction: Surrender charges are draconian measures to punish clients and make insurance companies wealthier. — Fiction!

Surrender charges are incorporated to discourage annuity holders from pulling money from accounts for frivolous reasons that do not constitute a serious need or emergency. This helps ensure that the full balance of the annuity will remain untouched and earning interest until the proper time when a retiree needs the annuity.

Moreover, the avoidance of paying surrender charges by pulling money out early allows the insurance carrier to invest money safely for a longer period of time thus enabling higher interest rates or returns while protecting all annuity owners interests.

Fact or Fiction: Fixed annuities can lock-in market-index gains and protect both principal and earnings in the account value. — Fact!

MarketFree™ Fixed annuities with a linked index option(s) always protect principal and interest by periodically locking in all principal and gains while providing the advantage of tax-deferral.

Fact or Fiction: Critics of annuities are mostly unbiased and factual. — Fiction!

MarketFree™ fixed and fixed index annuities have been the target of increasingly negative and biased criticisms as more and more baby boomers flock to guarantee financial security using these proven options. The securities industry has a longstanding bias against annuities since investors pull capital away from revenue producing stocks, bonds, and derivatives. There are some (financial writers) who do not sell securities directly, yet write in what would appear to be an unbiased manner. However many times, financial writers/contributors are indirectly compensated by the securities industry for offering a negative bias at the expense of annuities. They disseminate half-truths and misinformation adhering to a narrow bias that promotes the securities industry which in turn attracts targeted subscribers and/or advertisers.

While annuities are obviously not best for everyone, they are in fact a stable and sensible option for many retirees. Many armchair critics, however, speak against fixed annuities and fixed index annuities based on material misconceptions and blatant falsehoods perpetuated by the media and unfairly biased internet commentary.

Fact or Fiction: Annuities tie up money with no access until maturity. — Fiction!

Again, many opponents of annuities who are in competition for the dollars of investors nearing retirement are prone to convey the idea that the maturity date or surrender period of the contract for the annuity will prohibit individuals from having any penalty free access to account value until the annuity matures. However, this is untrue.

The maturity date simply means the amount of time the insurer will have applicable surrender charges. As previously stated during this time period, most annuities have many penalty-free withdrawal provisions including guaranteed lifetime income payouts. After the annuity matures beyond the surrender period, the annuity company still must meet its ongoing contractual guarantees. The maturity date only gives the annuity owner more flexibility with access to funds, 100 percent penalty free and surrender free.

MarketFree™ Fixed Annuities & Retirement

"Retirement is like a long vacation in Las Vegas. The goal is to enjoy it to the fullest, but not so fully that you run out of money."
-Jonathan Clements

Running out of money before the end of life has been a real concern for baby boomers and most retirees, especially since life expectancy continues to increase all the time. Individuals with retirement on their mind are understandably concerned that savings and income may not last. Indeed, many are searching for a retirement plan that will guarantee an income for the duration of life no matter how long the duration of life is. For this reason, fixed annuities are predictably increasing in popularity amongst this group of savers and investors.

Despite the volatile markets of recent years, fixed annuity owners have continued to earn on annuity allocations without risk of losing principal or earnings--a fact that applies to no other financial instruments out there.

No matter how the economy may fluctuate, retirees choosing fixed annuities enjoy interest earnings that are typically a couple of percentage points higher than banks. Although CDs provide a similar safety advantage yet their interest rates are typically lower than that of annuities and they cannot offer retirees a lifetime of guaranteed income as an option like annuities offer.

And because all annuities are tax deferred, money that would ordinarily be taxed is now earning interest instead of being paid to Uncle Sam first. Over an extended period of time in retirement, the earnings advantage is substantial. Tax is of course owed upon the withdrawal of funds from an annuity unless it is structured to be tax-free. Many individuals are in a lower tax bracket during retirement and therefore will not pay as much in tax compared to what might have been paid during a higher income stage in life.

Fixed annuities are considered to be investment-risk-free, the safety associated with a fixed annuity is substantial relative to the risks common with investment options offered by securities.

The most alluring aspect of fixed annuities for retirement-minded individuals is the security of knowing that the financial future will be predictable and as comfortable as hoped and planned for without unexpected financial loss catastrophes late in life.

Fixed Annuity Characteristics

- Lump-sum or periodic contributions;
- Invested in mostly high-quality A-AAA bonds, US treasuries and investment grade securities;
- No investment risk to clients. Insurance company assumes all risk;
- Guaranteed interest;
- Modest growth;
- 2 to 3.5 percent interest rates possible;
- One-to twenty-year maturity;
- Predictable, simple;
- Guaranteed future retirement income;
- No or low annual fees.

Fixed Annuity Benefits

- Safety - Backed by highly-rated and state-regulated--insurers;
- Tax Deferral - Tax-deferred growth;
- Higher Interest - Better interest rates typically than CDs;
- Life Insurance - Options for death benefit guarantees;
- Liquidity - Flexible withdrawal privileges;
- Unlimited Contributions - Unlike some other types of retirement accounts such as individual retirement accounts and 401(k)s;
- Inheritance - Pass money directly to heirs, bypassing probate;
- Lifetime Option - Income that cannot be outlived (annuitization or an income rider).

Fixed Annuity Performance

With recent fixed annuities, an annuity owner can typically expect earnings in the range of 2 to 3.5 percent. However, longer terms can generate interest gains compounded at 3 to 4 percent based on the current low rate environment. These rates are determined by the conditions of the annuity contract and the insurance company's ability to earn revenue based on their conservative portfolio of assets.

Fixed Deferred Annuities

The fixed deferred annuity is a retirement planning option that works well for those who are several years away from leaving the workforce or near retirement without an immediate income need. This type of annuity will benefit individuals who want growth or to continue contributing to retirement accounts without yet receiving payments from an annuity. Long-term deferral allows for the principal to continue gaining interest, tax deferred while the annuity grows for future income or wealth accumulation.

This particular annuity is considered a deferred annuity for two primary reasons. First, this annuity, unlike an immediate annuity, is not designed to provide an immediate stream of income. In fact, the annuity will continue to grow in deferral. This of course will increase the potential earnings from that annuity. If an income rider is chosen, the income base account can grow guaranteed at 4 to 8 percent during deferral. This ensures a high minimum guaranteed lifetime of future income payments. Secondly, the fixed deferred annuity has the added characteristic of being tax-deferred until the moment of withdrawal from the account. In essence, the funds incorporated into this type of account include retained tax proceeds which are also earning compounded interest for the annuity owner during the savings growth period. Although CDs are similarly structured to accumulate savings over an extended period of time, CDs are taxed annually decreasing the amount of funds earning interest.

Some fixed deferred annuities have another feature that makes them particularly appealing younger savers. This annuity may have a multi-premium option which allows the individual to make smaller contributions throughout the duration of the annuity. This is a convenient and practical feature for people who are unable to make a large initial investment. With this feature, annuity owners can grow smaller sums into much larger sums over time.

In case there is ever a need to withdraw from an annuity account, fixed deferred annuities like many other annuity types will allow for a percentage of the account to be withdrawn annually without penalties, typically 10 percent annually. However, withdrawals exceeding this contractual percentage will typically remain subject to fees and surrender penalties. Ten percent IRS penalties on earnings withdrawals prior to fifty-nine and a half years of age may also apply.

Fixed Deferred Annuity Characteristics

- Deferred fixed annuities first originated in the United States approximately one hundred years ago;
- They can be acquired via premium allocated by periodic, systematic, or lump sum payments;
- Deferral in fixed annuities allows the cash value, and if applicable, the income base value for income riders of the annuity to increase;
- After a period of deferral, a fixed annuity can produce more income;
- Deferred fixed annuities have the added advantage of tax deferral;
- They have annuitization, providing a lifetime of income;
- Deferred fixed annuities are mostly the opposite of immediate annuities since immediate annuities begin an income soon after they are funded in lump sum;
- Deferred fixed annuities are typically invested in high quality A-AAA government and investment-grade bonds;
- Fixed index deferred annuities are never invested into a market index; they are only using the index as a linked economic indicator in order to credit interest earned;
- A CD-style deferred fixed annuity is an annuity that can offer a multi-year interest guarantee. Only bank-issued CDs are FDIC insured;
- Deferred fixed annuities are creditor-protected in many states;
- Deferred fixed annuities are first guaranteed by the claims-paying ability of the insurer, and then each state has a State Insurance Guarantee Association (SIGA) with varying coverage limits.

MarketFree™ Fixed Annuity -- CD-Style

As suggested by the name, CD-style annuities have some

characteristics of traditional Certificates of Deposit and fixed annuities. However, there are distinct and substantial differences with some similarities that one needs to be aware of.

The contrasts between the CD-style annuities and traditional CD can make a significant difference in how a portfolio works for future income. This being said, take a moment to note the distinctions before determining the appropriate choice for a particular situation.

CD-style annuities, also known as multi-year-guarantee-annuities, share several attractive characteristics with other fixed annuities. For starters, both options guarantee the consumer a fixed rate of interest. Some fixed annuities will only assure this interest rate for a portion of the term, whereas CD-style annuities guarantee this rate for the entire guarantee period.

For instance, one may obtain an eight-year fixed annuity at 3.5 percent interest, but this rate may only be guaranteed for the first five years. The CD-style fixed annuity, however, will continue earning 3.5 percent for the full eight-year guarantee period.

Another added feature is that CD-style fixed annuities can be rolled over into other annuities without the transfer amount being taxed as income. Traditional CDs may not be transferred between accounts to avoid taxation and are not tax-deferred; they incur taxation annually.

With many CD-style fixed annuities, typically up to 10 percent of the initial investment plus interest can be liquidated annually without penalty; this is helpful in case of unforeseen circumstances. With traditional CDs, typically the entire account must be liquidated in order to remove amounts of any size. Ten percent early withdrawal tax penalties on earnings are applied to CD-style annuities for those under fifty-nine and one half years old.

CD-style fixed annuities provide the same income-for-life annuitization option that standard fixed annuities offer. CDs however, cannot provide this benefit because any stream of income ends once CD account values are depleted.

And unlike CD-style fixed annuities issued by insurance companies, traditional CDs are only issued by banks and are insured by the FDIC for up to

$250,000 per account. On the other hand, CD-style annuities are covered by the claims paying ability of the issuing insurance company and a State Insurance Guarantee Association (SIGA) with coverage varying by state--which should not be compared to FDIC which has the full backing of the U.S. government. The amount of SIGA coverage limits on annuities is dependent upon the state in which the annuity is issued, typically ranging between $100,000 and $500,000.

Fixed Annuity Alternatives

There are many alternatives to fixed annuities and some obviously may serve specific financial purposes better than others. Likewise, there are many alternatives that will not help with specific objectives at all. In fact, the wrong investment can obviously hurt rather than help.

To achieve important financial objectives, it may be possible that a diversification using several alternative allocations will work best to secure some retirement plans. In large part, it is rarely the investment itself that is at fault but rather poor use of that particular investment or insurance product. An investment that could be a financial disadvantage to one person may be the best financial instrument to provide for the future of another.

Successful financial planning strategies are unique to each person; considering circumstances, needs and desires. An experienced financial advisor understands this and will evaluate a client's financial condition independently and without unfair bias toward one investment or another.

If one should choose to tackle retirement planning without help, consider many of the pertinent factors before making a decision. Remember that everyone will need the services of a licensed advisor or agent to fund an annuity. In fact, it is a state enforced requirement regulating annuity purchases only through licensed agents.

While getting advice from relatives and neighbors can be beneficial when purchasing consumer goods or something of that nature, retirement options are another matter entirely. Unlike buying a car or household items, ones financial condition may not be remotely similar to that of friends and family.

Doing all the homework in investigating all of the options carefully is one of the keys. It cannot be emphasized enough that one's entire retirement future succeeds or fails upon the decisions made or not made in a timely manner.

MarketFree™ Fixed annuity alternatives to consider:

- Certificates of Deposit
- Money Markets
- T-Bills
- Savings Accounts
- Treasury Inflation Protected Securities
- U.S. Government Bonds
- Municipal Bonds
- Investment-Grade Bonds
- Junk Bonds
- Bond Funds
- Bond ETFs
- Preferred Stock
- Common Stock
- Managed Money Accounts
- Stock Options
- Real Estate Investment Trusts
- Mutual Funds
- Exchange Traded Funds
- Unit Investment Trusts
- Closed-End Funds
- Modified Endowment Contracts
- Investment-Grade Life Insurance
- REITS
- Life Settlements
- Pre-Issued Annuities ™

Fixed Annuity Disadvantages

As stated previously, ones views on the advantages or disadvantages of fixed annuities are directly impacted by an individual's particular financial perspective and circumstance. Certain features of this type of annuity may be unattractive for some and the most appealing option for many others.

For example, people who had retirement funds allocated into fixed annuities during the Great recession of 2008-2009 were very likely pleased when the account balance grew and remained intact. Other folks with less stable investments lost portions of, or in extreme cases, most or even all their retirement savings.

The fixed annuity performed exactly as hoped and expected.

Here is a list of fixed annuity disadvantages. It will be up to each one to decide how advantageous or unattractive a particular option is.

- Ten percent tax penalty on earnings withdrawals prior to fifty-nine and a half years of age;
- Early withdrawal penalties or surrender charges when withdrawing in excess of the allowable portion; a 10 percent surrender-free withdrawal annually;
- Ordinary income tax owed on earnings during the withdrawal or income payout stage with the exception of tax free annuities;
- Last in first out (LIFO) tax requirement so earnings are taxed first unless annuitization takes place, then an IRS formula to determine the tax exclusion ratio is used;
- Fixed annuities are not FDIC insured;
- Fixed annuities are boring and lack higher earning potential;
- Standard fixed annuities may not keep up with inflation.

Choosing the Best Fixed Annuity

Finding the best fixed annuity offered by competing insurance companies is determined by factors that are particular to the specific financial needs and objectives of an individual. Financial goals, assets, age, health, and income needs are but a few of the considerations that will have to be examined carefully before committing to any one company or type of annuity. In other words, there is no such thing as the best fixed annuity - at least not one that is best for everyone. The fixed annuity that suits a particular person might prove financially disastrous for one's neighbor. This is not a situation where one size fits all.

Choosing the best fixed annuity can be an overwhelming process if there is no clarity of what will be needed to reach realistic retirement goals. Even individuals who have clearly mapped objectives may need a little help making the correct final choice. For this reason, many people feel more comfortable finalizing annuity setup with the assistance of an experienced financial professional.

One may not find the perfect annuity which can satisfy the entirety of a financial plan, but broader knowledge on annuity variations helps in selecting one or a combination of annuities structured skillfully to achieve clearly defined financial objectives.

One should take a moment or two reflecting on the financial aspects of the future which are of greatest concern. Construct a list of these items. Once the list is completed, consider thoroughly each item and prioritize in the order of most importance. This gives an individual the clarity as to what would be the most appropriate annuity or annuities to ladder that would meet future financial concerns.

Again, if at any time the choices are not clear and comfortable or one is less than confident, consult an expert to help customize a portfolio using annuities that will reach one's objectives, making certain that the highest priorities are being met, thus, giving one the level of confidence to move forward.

This list may help one determine some of the factors worth considering when exploring the many annuity variations, to wit:

- High independent ratings for safety concerns;
- High-interest crediting for growth;
- Generous payout percentages for income;
- Liquidity for emergency cash needs;
- Fair surrender periods and fair surrender charges;
- Additional benefits such as payouts for long-term care, terminal illness, and death benefits;
- Flexible income riders that allow both lifetime income and the ability to pass any remaining account value to heirs;
- Index options for higher earnings-growth potential;

- Better index strategies for higher interest-earning growth potential;
- A bonus, only if all retirement objectives are satisfied first.

Video: MarketFree™ Fixed Annuities Advisors Love or Hate Them

Click & Watch this video to find out...

Video URL: http://annuityguys.com/marketfree-annuities-why-advisors-love-them-or-hate-them

QR Code for smart phones:

Chapter 5: Variable Annuities

"I hope to never have to sell another encyclopedia. With my new license, selling variable annuities should be a snap."

"I've got all the money I'll ever need, if I die by four o'clock."
-Henry Youngman

Case Study 4 -- Jim

Although the market has had its ups and downs over the past few years, Jim was advised by his financial advisor in 2008 to place a portion of his retirement funds totaling $200,000 into a variable annuity.

Upon hearing all of the negative news in the media during the recent Great Recession about the stock market, underlying investments in variable annuities, and high fees; Jim's daughter, Cindy, explained that she was quite upset with her father's advisor for placing her father's retirement funds into a variable annuity.

Two years after placing his $200,000 into the variable annuity and after the stock market was down approximately 40 percent, Jim had passed away. However, after comparing other investments that her father's funds could have been invested in, Cindy, upon further examination was not so upset anymore. This is because after her father's passing, it was actually determined that if Jim had placed his $200,000 directly into stocks or mutual funds. His heirs would probably have only received about $120,000.

But since Jim's funds were placed in an annuity with a guaranteed death benefit, his beneficiaries instead would at least receive back his original investment of $200,000.

Variable Annuity History

Variable annuities have remained a prominent fixture in retirement plans since the 1970s. Variable deferred annuities were first introduced as an aid for educators to increase savings while potentially earning higher investment returns to protect against growing inflation. This annuity was initiated by TIAA-CREF around 1952 and in 1959, the United States Supreme Court deemed that variable annuities would be subject to federal securities regulation.

The following year, in 1960, the very first non-qualified variable annuity became available on the market. This opened the sales of variable annuities up to individual investors who were looking for a way to save for retirement and yet get potentially larger returns than those offered by fixed annuity contracts.

By 1980, guaranteed minimum death benefits were introduced. And soon afterwards, in 1982, the Tax Equity and Fiscal Responsibility Act allowed annuities to keep a tax-deferred status. This act was also responsible for allowing annuities to retain the exclusion ratio that treats annuity income benefit payments as a partial return of principal and a partial return of taxable earnings. It also changed how annuity withdrawals are taxed; when withdrawals are made, principal comes out last and interest or earnings must be withdrawn first. This meant that an annuitant would be taxed on the growth portion of the funds in the annuity contract first. Also known as Last In First Out (LIFO).

As the popularity of annuities continued to grow, the National Association for Variable Annuities was formed in 1991. This organization's purpose is to promote the knowledge of variable annuities not only to the members of the group but also to the general public as a whole.

Because the variable annuity is a combination of both insurance and investments, this annuity is regulated by state insurance and investment regulatory authorities. Since its introduction, the variable investment-oriented annuity has grown in popularity especially for younger professionals seeking tax-deferred, moderate to aggressive growth strategies (Only slowing in recent years with the popularity of fixed index- or hybrid style-annuities).

All Annuities are Variable -- Right?

Variable annuities typically appeal to individuals who are willing to take market risks in order to increase returns. Many of these investors are still several years from retirement and hope to recover, if they have market losses, and be way ahead over the course of time.

Unfortunately, variable annuities may also be appealing to those who have started late preparing for retirement. Many of these individuals consider the variable annuity a solution to increasing savings prior to leaving the workforce by taking more risk with a bit of an income or death benefit safety-net. Variable annuities are market sensitive and the initial principal invested is typically guaranteed as a death benefit.

One of the common stereotypes surrounding annuities is that "all annuities fall into the variable annuity category of high fees, high surrenders, and investment risk to principal". This unfortunate misconception has been suggested by many seemingly unbiased investment analysts, commentators, or brokers who wish to deter potential clients from creating a financial plan that may include MarketFree™ annuities instead of securities for growth and income.

However, there are many types of annuities with features as varied as the people who choose to own them. An independent financial advisor who specializes in structuring annuities in a balanced portfolio can help with the decision as to which of the many types of annuities may help best to accomplish specific financial objectives.

Fact or Fiction - Know the Truth!

Fact or Fiction: If I invest my money into a variable annuity, I am more likely to increase my retirement savings. — Fiction!

Not necessarily. Variable annuities are market sensitive and are therefore as volatile as the stock market itself. No one can predict with certainty how the market will perform from year to year. In that respect, owning variable annuities can be a bit like gambling. For younger investors with, say, twenty years or more to stay invested, the odds are better for the variable annuity to outperform safer investments.

Fact or Fiction: Although variable annuities guarantee a death benefit, they cannot guarantee principal or earnings. — Fact!

Principal and earnings are always at risk in variable annuity. Added to this risk, one of the primary criticisms leveled at variable annuities is the high fees that are consistently associated with them. In a poor-performing market, the added weight of high annual fees could potentially eat away at account value and substantially increase losses.

Fact or Fiction: All annuities are like variable annuities. — Fiction!

This is a myth. In fact, almost 40 percent of recent annuities purchased are fixed annuities-- offering a guarantee of fixed minimum interest rates and future protection against loss of principal and earnings. Fixed annuities feature no- or low-fees. Variable annuities have the advantage of unlimited upside market potential that must be weighed against the downside risk to principal.

Fact or Fiction: Insurance guarantees offered by variable annuities offer no real value to the annuity owner. — Fiction!

This, too, is a myth. Death benefits and living benefits offered by variable annuities can actually help to protect a retiree's retirement assets against downturns in the market. This is especially valuable at a time when, in many other types of retirement savings such as 401(k), values have dropped significantly. And, although there is an added cost for these benefits the value they provide can be thought of as similar to other types of insurance such as car or homeowner policies.

In other words, even though annuity owners may never need the protection, the owner would be in a very bad way if it was needed but not selected.

Fact or Fiction: Variable annuities are never a good investment for older annuity owners. — Fiction!

Although variable annuities may not be an appropriate investment for everyone, they should not be dismissed as being bad for all older investors. This is because every person's situation is different. Some older investors can afford to have additional funds placed at risk for the potential rewards. In addition, because time in retirement can span over twenty or more years, a variable annuity could offer some much needed investment growth to help as a hedge against inflation.

Fact or Fiction: Variable annuities lock up assets for an indefinite period of time. — Fiction!

The truth is that most variable annuities today offer investors access to at least a portion of account value annually, usually 10 percent. And an annuity owner is normally allowed to do so without incurring a penalty. Then after typically six to ten years, all surrender charges end.

Fact or Fiction: It is a bad idea to hold a variable annuity inside of a tax-deferred retirement account such as an IRA. — Fiction!

This is also a myth. In truth, the guarantees offered by the variable annuity as well as the guaranteed income options can actually make this a viable investment/retirement approach in certain circumstances.

Where some investors may have vast knowledge about financial issues, the majority of individuals would benefit much more by allowing a trained financial professional to guide one through the maze of different options, features, and benefits of variable annuities or annuities in general to ensure that the right annuity or annuities are chosen based on the investor's unique needs.

Variable Annuity Features

Variable deferred annuities offer a large and diversified collection of features combined with an attractive tax-deferral wrapper. Because this annuity has direct market growth investment potential, some advisors position the variable deferred annuity as a means in which to protect against rising inflation.

Variable deferred annuities have similarities to 401(k) plans and other employee-sponsored retirement plans. However, unlike those plans, variable deferred annuities do not have an IRS limit on the amount of savings one can contribute to his or her retirement account. This has obviously been an attractive alternative for certain high income individuals.

Nevertheless, both employee-sponsored retirement plans and variable deferred annuities have been criticized in the media for some time since they both are known to have high fees that eat away at overall return stifling the growth of these retirement investment plans.

Additionally, variable deferred annuities have not performed well in more recent time periods due to the volatility of the stock market in the last ten to fifteen years. Compared with popular stock market index funds, the variable annuity fees are usually higher by at least a couple of percentage points or more.

Variable Annuity Benefits

- Growth oriented earnings from equity returns;
- Death benefit protection on the initial investment;
- Liquidity provisions;
- Potential for higher investment performance - no limits on tax deferred investment amounts;
- No minimum required distributions on non-IRA assets;
- Avoids probate;
- Has tax deferral;
- Living benefit income riders;
- Annuitization options;
- Potential for a bonus.

Variable Annuity Performance

Variable annuity performance is consistent with that of the securities market which has not done very well over the last decade or so. To get a fair representation one may want to consider the last fifty years. The return potential with investments in an index fund mirroring the S&P 500 or perhaps the Dow Jones Industrials would have averaged in the vicinity of 8 percent compounded annually over fifty years!

Variable annuity investment performance along with tax deferral can return impressive results in certain time periods. However, the market of 1999 through 2009 was not kind to variable annuity investors. The combination of poor market conditions and high variable annuity fees stifled and even sent retirement plans plunging deep into negative territory during this period, becoming the antithesis of an inflationary hedge.

Approximations of fees that are customary on variable annuities are as follows:

- Administrative: 0.25 percent
- Mortality: 0.75 percent
- Income rider: 0.75 to 2 percent
- Enhanced Death Benefit: 0.75 percent
- Underlying Investment Expense: 1.5 percent

Based on the above fees, minimum fees on a stripped-out variable annuity are around 2 percent and a fully featured variable annuity may run as high as 5 percent. In short, if variable annuity investments are down 20 percent and additional fees are included, the variable annuity is automatically down 25 percent. In this case, fees could compose around 20 percent of the loss that's incurred. This can be devastating to the principal exponentially retarding future appreciation.

Variable Annuity Alternatives

There are numerous alternatives to variable annuities and some may serve retiree financial goals better than others. On the contrary, there are also many variable annuity alternatives that may not help retirement financial objectives at all. In fact, investing in the wrong vehicle can actually hurt overall financial goals.

Just like any other investment, in order to achieve important retirement financial objectives, individuals should diversify holdings across different investment vehicles. In most cases, it is not just one single investment that will help one to achieve goals but rather an overall retirement strategy.

Having a successful financial planning strategy requires that each individual determines his or her long-, intermediate-, and short-term financial goals. Then it becomes clearer which financial instruments are best suited for helping to get an individual well positioned financially for a successful retirement.

It is imperative when using variable annuities--or any type of investment vehicle--that each person does his or her homework and truly understands the full range of options available.

Some alternatives to consider in addition to variable annuities:

- Fixed Annuities
- Hybrid Index Annuities
- Mutual Funds

- Stocks
- CDs
- Bonds
- Money Market Accounts
- Savings Accounts
- Exchange Traded Funds (ETFs)
- Real Estate Investment Trusts (REITs)
- Unit Investment Trusts (UITs)
- Investment-Grade Life Insurance

Variable Annuity Disadvantages

- Higher expenses, sometimes as much as 4-5 percent or more;
- Taxation as ordinary income upon distribution;
- No step-up in cost basis for heirs tax advantage;
- Limited liquidity;
- Considerable limitations in investment choices;
- Not considered a substitute for life insurance.

Choosing the Best Variable Annuities

Variable annuities have held the distinction of having the highest potential growth among annuities. With the bear market of 2000 through 2003 and the Great Recession of 2008 through 2009, it became painfully apparent that variable annuities also have the greatest risk of loss.

Due to the market lows of 1999 to 2009, variable annuities have typically fell behind fixed annuities, and fixed index annuities.

In addition, investing outside of a variable annuity into a mutual fund or Index fund equivalent to the variable annuity subaccounts would produce better results than the variable annuity as a direct result of higher fees that are built into variable annuities.

However, variable annuities may still be the best option for someone seeking tax deferral and potential market gains. Nevertheless, it remains impossible to bestow the title of "best variable annuity" on any one variation.

This title, actually, can only be determined based upon someone's unique financial situation with the advantage of evaluating the variable annuity by the use of *hindsight being 20/20.*

It is common knowledge that all investments including variable annuities are based on unpredictable future performance and past performance cannot be used as an indicator to predict future results.

Video: <u>Variable Annuity vs. Hybrid Annuity</u>

<u>Click & Watch this video to find out which one fits you best...</u>

Video URL: <u>http://annuityguys.com/variable-annuities-compared-to-hybrid-annuities</u>

QR Code for smart phones:

Chapter 6:

MarketFree™ Fixed Index Annuities

"Honey, we definitely saved enough for our retirement if we can just get the timing to work out at the end."

"The safe way to double your money is to fold it over once and put it in your pocket." -Frank Hubbard

Case Study 5 -- Mike and Lisa

When Mike, a sixty-five-year-old retiree, called to take action on designing and implementing a financial plan a few years back, one of his long-term objectives was to provide a comfortable retirement for himself and his wife Lisa.

Ever since he had retired, Mike had become quite concerned about the safety of his retirement assets. He did not want what he had worked so hard for to be lost in a market downturn; however, he also understood that he would need to supplement his other retirement income in order to maintain the lifestyle that they both had become accustomed to. And one of Mike's primary goals was to structure an inflation-hedged income stream that neither he nor his wife would be able to outlive.

After going over Mike's retirement assets as well as his intended goals, it was suggested that he consider fixed index annuities with an income riders offering joint payouts. (This type of annuity is a fixed annuity that has its interest linked to a popular market index that will lock in the interest earnings up to a stated cap each year, when there is a gain in that index. Yet, these annuities can not incur any negative index return when the stock market tumbles which protect the annuity from any decrease in value resulting from market losses).

Using $400,000 of Mike's $900,000 in retirement funds, the couple decided to go with MarketFree™ fixed index annuities laddered to hedge against inflation. Now, with the joint payout options they selected, Mike and Lisa will be able to have an increasing income that neither of them can outlive. In addition, any account value they have not used for income can be passed to their three adult children as heirs since they will remain in majority control of their annuity asset.

Fixed Index Annuity History

Fixed index annuities were originally introduced in the United States approximately eighteen years ago as an alternative to the volatility of mutual funds. These annuities allow the holders to participate in growth linked to market indexes, yet prevent the risk of loss to the annuity owner's principal in years when these popular and sometimes lesser known indices produce a loss. Due to this feature, money flowed rapidly into these types of annuities during the Great Recession of 2008-2009. And, to the surprise of many analysts according to the 2009 and 2010 Wharton Study, these index annuities have proven to deliver higher annuity account growth than the growth of the market index they were linked to over specific five-and ten-year recent time periods.

Understanding Fixed Index Annuities (FIA)

A fixed index annuity is a type of deferred fixed annuity that earns interest based on being linked to an external equity measure such as a popular market or commodity index. Two of the more common indices used are the S&P 500 or the Dow Jones Industrial Average. Dividends may or may not be added to the index return for the interest calculation formula.

The value of an index annuity will not vary from day to day. This annuity has a stable account balance interest that is typically added and locked in-once a year or after a specified period of time usually on an anniversary date. When an individual purchases a fixed index annuity, the annuity purchaser is actually allocating principal/premium to an insurance contract rather than purchasing shares of stock in an equity index.

Index annuities differ from other types of annuities because of the way that they credit interest to the account value. For example, while some fixed annuities will only credit interest that is calculated at a daily preset rate in the contract, others credit interest rates that are set annually as the current rate by the issuing insurance company. Index annuities will credit interest using a predetermined formula that is based on changes in a specified market index. This formula will determine how the interest is calculated, and how much interest the annuity holder will receive, if any-- when interest is paid will depend upon the elected index strategy of a particular fixed index annuity. Many prefer this fixed annuity--index option, since it gives some upside market potential with no downside market risk allowing the potential for higher interest earnings based on an objective method for determining a fair rate of interest that is applied and locked into the annuity account value.

Fact or Fiction - Know the Truth!

Although there are many positive aspects to a fixed index annuity, there are still some myths that surround these financial instruments. Therefore, it is a good idea to know the difference of what is fact and what is fiction.

Fact or Fiction: Index annuities are a bad financial planning tool. — Fiction!

The truth is that index annuities offer interest that is linked to the upside growth of popular stock indexes without the downside risks of loss in those same market indexes. In addition, index annuities are both insured and protected assets and they can be used as part of a predictable and comprehensive financial plan.

They are also excellent retirement and estate planning financial tools due to the fact that they are safe, avoid probate, and are tax deferred or tax free if used as a Roth IRA. In fact, these types of annuities are very suitable for the funds that should not be put at risk of market loss such as allocations made to establish a safe retirement account since principal, earnings, and income can be guaranteed against market losses.

Fact or Fiction: Index annuities are expensive and they pay a large commission at the expense of clients. — Fiction!

Some financial advisors and supposedly unbiased commentators discredit index annuities unfairly. Actually, in contrast, they have no fees other than an optional income rider fee of normally less than 1 percent.

Commissions are typically much lower for indexed annuities than what is earned on securities investments over ten years or less. However, this undeserved attack is mostly from ignorance or because these products offer less overall profit for the securities industry.

Unlike variable annuities, a fixed index annuity does not deduct mortality expenses, administrative fees, sales charges, and management fees.

Fact or Fiction: Individuals always receive a lower return on MarketFree™ index annuities than on other types of annuities or investments. —

Fiction!

In fact, index annuities have been producing moderate returns since the very first one was created in 1995, being much more stable than securities and other investments throughout the same time period. Many have outperformed popular stock indexes considerably during the first decade and beyond in the twenty-first century.

Fact or Fiction: Fixed index annuities are not fully liquid investments and they also have surrender charges. — Fact!

Unlike some assets that are traded in the open market, fixed index annuities are private contracts which are similar in that regard to nonnegotiable certificates of deposit. Thus, fixed index annuities are not traded in the open marketplace and therefore they have no market price. So using this definition of liquidity would be unfair.

In addition, unlike some stocks and bonds--but similar to a bank CD--a fixed index annuity can be easily cashed in with its issuer at any time and at a price that is formulaically pre-specified in the contract. In fact in this scenario, there is essentially always has a willing buyer.

Both CDs and fixed index annuities have surrender penalties for premature withdrawal or early surrender; however, both are easily convertible into cash. In addition, in the case of some CDs the early withdrawal penalty could depend upon how early they are liquidated. However, with other CDs, the penalty may be fixed regardless of how early they are cashed in.

In the case of fixed index annuities, the cost of an early surrender penalty is nearly always relative to how early the surrender occurs and the amount withdrawn. Typically, a 10 percent withdrawal is allowed each year without a surrender penalty, and some fixed index annuity contracts even allow more than 10 percent annually.

The 10 percent withdrawal is considerably more than what an investor may be able to withdraw from CDs or treasury inflation-protected bonds without being subjected to penalties or potential losses of principal due to bond price fluctuations. Even potentially more so when a securities portfolio includes stocks and corporate bonds that may be caught in a downward cycle when money is needed.

A fixed index annuity technically is simply a fixed annuity that also offers an optional index feature. And, in addition to having fixed annuity safety of principal and a fixed interest rate, it also has an optional interest-crediting method that typically uses a popular external market index in determining the amount of interest to be applied after a specified time period of usually one year.

In addition, all fixed index annuities offer tax deferral and thus they have no requirement of income tax or IRS reporting until the time of withdrawal. This is a nice advantage over other alternatives such as mutual funds, CDs, or dividend paying stocks, when individuals are considering a long-term tax friendly retirement solution.

A long-term fixed index annuity has the potential to easily outperform certificates of deposit, bonds, and treasuries. Retirees should also realize that a fixed index annuity was never designed to outperform popular stock indices. However, most did just that for the first ten years of the twenty-first century. And keeping funds earning compound interest that otherwise would have been paid out in tax over time is always a huge advantage as well. Fixed index annuities also have numerous other benefits (to be explained further in this chapter) that are of importance for retirement planning.

Fixed Index Annuity Features

In light of the recent severe stock market downturn, investors are more concerned than ever about the loss of principal. Many retirees and pre-retirees lost large percentages of net worth--and many do not have time to make up those losses. This can have a serious negative impact on most lifestyles in retirement years.

A fixed index annuity can provide a way for individuals to help lock in market gains, while at the same time preventing one from losing hard-earned principal and interest. The earnings or interest in a fixed index annuity are tied to stock market-like performance from certain popular indices. What this means is that the annuities' interest added to the annuity account value will be based on the performance of specific securities such as those in the S&P

500 index.

A fixed index annuity is directly linked to the performance of this type of a market index, yet without the worry of participating in the actual stock or equity investments themselves. Therefore, with this indexing option, annuity holders are able to participate in a well-diversified passive strategy having a link to the market and its potential gains without being subject to the potential downfalls of the actual market. As a result, these annuities can enjoy the guarantees and the safety of principal and interest earnings even while they are linked to the growth in the market. One thing to keep in mind, however, is that fixed index annuities do not reflect identically or pay out the full upside earning potential of the selected index.

In addition, a fixed index annuity can provide its holders with the best features of a traditional fixed annuity--the guarantee of principal, earnings and income--without subjecting holders to market losses while enjoying some upside market potential.

Unlike most mutual funds or stocks where an investor's account balance can fluctuate and lose value due to market performance, with a fixed index annuity the cash (referred to as premium) that is allocated plus locked in interest on specified anniversary dates is guaranteed to never decrease due to any market loss.

Moreover, all annuity values accumulate on a tax-deferred basis until withdrawn and a fixed index annuity is no exception. This allows the annuity holder's money to accumulate even faster because it is earning compound interest on funds that would have otherwise been paid to good ole Uncle Sam as a tax obligation.

Also similar to other types of annuities, a fixed index annuity can provide owners with a guaranteed lifetime income stream. Fixed index annuity holders have the ability to choose from several different income rider--income payout options or income--annuitization options.

Also typical in most other types of annuities, a fixed index annuity will allow the holder to take some type of penalty-free withdrawals--typically up to 10 percent of the initial premium, or in many contracts, 10 percent of the full account value--each year after the first anniversary of the annuity contract.

Fixed Index Annuity Benefits

A fixed index annuity essentially can offer the best of two worlds: a guarantee of the principal amount with the potential for market-linked growth, while at the same time having no risk of loss to principal from downturns in a selected market index. Additional benefits of fixed index annuities include:

- Tax deferral - Tax-deferred growth;
- Safety - Backing of high-rated insurers and state-regulated insurance companies;
- Potential for higher interest - Better interest rate potential than certificates of deposit or other basic fixed annuities;
- Life insurance - Death benefit options;
- Liquidity - Contractual right for flexible withdrawal options;
- Ability to make unlimited contribution amounts;
- Inheritance - Ability to pass funds directly to heirs and bypass probate;
- Income - Provides a guaranteed income by annuitization or an optional income rider for income that cannot be outlived.

Income Riders & Contractual Guarantees -
"Absolute guarantees, No-moving parts."

Fixed Index-/Hybrid-Annuities--allow for upside potential while having specific moving parts in addition to absolute contractual guarantees.

Income Rider - addendum to an annuity contract guaranteeing a future lifetime income plus additional specified benefits in some income riders (this is an absolute contractual guarantee).

MarketFree™ Index Annuity Specifics

1. Annuity Owner Remains in majority control of the annuity's cash account value during the surrender term and has 100% control after the surrender term at maturity.

---

2. Full account value of the cash account passes on to heirs with no surrender or penalty charge.

3. Guaranteed growth for income in deferral guaranteeing a minimum future income.

Example: Initial Premium $100,000 + 5% bonus guaranteed growth of 7.2 percent deferred for ten years = $210,000 income account value producing a guaranteed income of $12,600 per year at age 70 with a single life payout.

4. Payout percentages from the income account are based on age and a single or joint income need.

Example: Age seventy - single payout, 6 percent or joint payout, 5.5 percent

5. Fees for riders can be based on the cash or income account value and are paid out of the cash account. Fees typically range from half of one percent (.5%) to one and a quarter percent (1.25%). This does not reduce the guaranteed growth of the income account also referred to as an annual rollup or income floor.

6. May have a death benefit allowing the income account, if it is larger than the cash account, to be distributed to heirs over a five-year period.

7. May have an increasing income as an inflation hedge.

8. May have a Long Term Care Benefit.

Index Strategy Moving Parts

Index examples: *S&P 500, *Dow Jones Industrial, *Trader Vic -- (*Commodities Strategy);

Uncapped Index - the full percentage of earnings growth on an index to be applied as interest to the cash account value and income account value if it exceeds the contractually guaranteed growth.

Cap - limits the percentage of earnings growth on an index to be applied as interest to the cash account value and income account value.

•**Positive Example:** 3% Cap *S&P index is up 10% for the year interest credited is 3%.

•**Negative Example:** 3 % Cap *S&P index is down 10% for the year interest credited is 0%.

Spread - a fee based on a percentage subtracted first, only when index earnings exist. Any earnings are applied as interest to the cash account value and income account value. The spread is never applied if there are no interest earnings.

•**Positive Example:** 3% Spread *S&P index is up 10% for the year interest credited is 7%.

•**Negative Example:** 3% Spread *S&P index is down 10% for the year interest credited is 0% the spread is no longer applicable.

Participation - allows a percentage of index growth to be applied as interest to the cash account value and income account value.

•**Positive Example:** 30% Participation *S&P index is up 10% for the year interest credited is 3%.

•**Negative Example:** 30% Participation *S&P index is down 10% for the year interest credited is 0%.

Average - allows the average index growth to be applied as interest to the cash account value and income account value over a specified period of time.

•**Positive Example:** *S&P index is at 100 at the beginning of the year and it fluctuates up and down between 110 and 100 for the year with six months of the index being at 110 and six months at 100. The average annual interest credited is 5%.

•**Formula:** (110+100+110+100+110+100+110+100+110+100+110+100)
=1260/12=105-100 = 5%

•**Negative Example:** *S&P index is at 100 at the beginning of the year and it fluctuates up and down between 100 and 90 for the year with six months of the index being at 100 and six months at 90. The average annual interest credited is 0%.

•**Formula:** (90+100+90+100+90+100+90+100+90+100+90+100)
=1140/12=95-100 = -5%

Capped Monthly Sum or Average - allows for adding together each months index growth limited by a cap to the upside with no cap limit to the downside in any month. The downside is subtracted from the cumulative total. Cumulative earnings are applied as interest to the cash account value and income account value over a specified period of time.

- **Positive Example:** *S&P index is up 12% for the year, however; six months were 0% earnings and six months were 2% earnings each. The monthly cap is 1%, the annual interest credited is 6%.

  - **Formula:** (0% x 6 months = 0%) + (1% x 6 months = 6%) = 6%

- **Negative Example:** *S&P index is up 12% for the year; however, six months were negative 2% earnings and six months were 4% earnings each. The monthly cap is 1%. The annual interest credited is 0%.

  - **Formula:** (-2% x 6 months = -12%) + (1% x 6 months = 6%) = -6%

Blend - combining a specified percentage of account value to an uncapped index for earnings growth with a specified percentage of account value based on a fixed interest portion. Then add all gains and any losses to determine the interest to be applied to the cash account value and income account value.

- **Positive Example:** *S&P index is up 10% for the year; 50% of the blend is an uncapped index and 50% of the blend is a fixed rate of 2%. The annual interest credited is 6%.

  - **Formula:** (10% x 50% = 5%) + (2% x 50%= 1%) = 6%

- **Negative Example:** *S&P index is down 10% for the year; 50% of the blend is an uncapped index and 50% of the blend is a fixed rate of 2%. The annual interest credited is 0%.

  - **Formula:** (-10% x 50% = -5%)+(2% x 50%= 1%) = -4%

Fees - are typically associated with optional riders. Fees are subtracted from cash value accounts not affecting income guarantee accounts. It may reduce principal in years with no interest earnings. (Some rider fees are specified as a spread and do not lower cash account value in years with no interest earnings).

Index Strategies & Various Time Period...

Combinations using the index components described above:

- Annual Point-to-Point with a Cap
- Annual Point-to-Point Average with a Spread
- Annual Point-to-Point Capped Monthly Average or Monthly Sum
- Point-to-Point with a Participation Rate
- Biennial Point-to-Point with a Biennial Cap
- Quadrennial Point-to-Point with a Quadrennial Blend
- Five Year Point to Point with an Uncapped Commodity Index

Index Annuity Performance

The performance of fixed index annuities will essentially vary with the market. This is because the interest-crediting options are linked to a specific index. The interest earned on index annuities can be somewhat difficult to estimate, due to the fact that they track volatile indices such as the S&P 500, longer-term growth can be at least estimated. Typically, most index annuities can earn 3 to 5 percent in this present low interest rate environment.

It is important to note that since an index annuity will never lose capital, it is always moving forward and locking in the previous specified period of interest earnings. Therefore, during a recession, the index annuity will not spiral downward; ironically, it actually has more potential with market volatility since it resets at the new low and index growth starts compounding again based on the new locked in account value (which includes principal and earnings as the new locked in account value) for the next year's gains! This is how the FIA handily outperformed many popular indices from 1999 to 2010.

Fixed Index Annuity Disadvantages

With all of the positive features of fixed index annuities, there are a few things to be aware of what could be considered disadvantages in certain situations.

First, fixed index annuities can be difficult to understand. Due to this, sometimes retirees may fall victim to sales representatives who may not completely disclose all of the important aspects of these unique annuities.

Another thing, a fixed index annuity could tie up a portion of an owner's money for eight to fifteen years potentially. Although, there is typically a penalty-free withdrawal provision of normally 10 percent, this still means that a majority of the funds will be subject to a surrender penalty should the annuity holder need his or her money in full right away. Surrender fees reduce steadily as the contract moves toward maturity.

Therefore, it is important to be certain that the funds used for a fixed index annuity are those that need not be withdrawn in an excessive amount for the near future. These funds should be positioned for a long-term secure retirement foundation.

Choosing a Fixed Index Annuity

There are many factors to consider when choosing to allocate premium into a fixed index annuity. Keep in mind that there are no perfect Index-/Hybrid-Annuities that meet every objective this is where prioritizing retirement objectives with an annuity specialist can make all the difference.

Some of the more important considerations include:

- High ratings for safety;
- High interest crediting to allow for growth;
- Reasonable surrender periods;
- Additional benefits such as increased payouts for long-term care or access to cash for terminal illness;
- Flexible income riders that allow both lifetime income and the ability to pass any remaining account value to heirs;
- More indexing options for higher growth potential;
- Reasonable or no annual fees;
- Higher deferred growth of the income base;
- Flexible joint survivor income guarantees;
- Availability of the income base for a death benefit;

Choosing the best fixed index annuity will depend largely on an individual's needs and situation. For example, while this type of annuity may be ideal for one person's planning, it could be a bad choice for a neighbor with a large pension and minimal retirement assets.

It is also important to note that no one particular fixed index annuity will give its owner everything that is desired for retirement. Therefore, it is important to prioritize all retirement needs - from most important to least important, and then match up those needs with the fixed index annuities that best match the overall highest priority retirement objectives.

*Disclosure: All examples are hypothetical for conceptual for educational purposes. The Dow Jones Industrial Average is a price-weighted index of 30 actively traded blue-chip stocks. The NASDAQ Composite Index is an unmanaged, market-weighted index of all over-the-counter common stocks traded on the National Association of Securities Dealers Automated Quotation System. The Standard & Poor's 500 (S&P 500) is an unmanaged group of securities considered to be representative of the stock market in general. It is not possible to invest directly in an index. TVI, TVI Index, Trader Vic Index, EAM Partners L.P., and EAM are trademarks of EAM Partners L.P. ("EAM"). The Trader Vic Index™ was created and is owned by EAM. EAM developed, maintains and is the sole party responsible for the methodology that is employed in connection with the Trader Vic Index™. The Barclays Capital U.S. Aggregate Bond Index is comprised of U.S. investment-grade, fixed-rate bond market securities, including government, government agency, corporate, and mortgage-backed securities. Barclays Capital and Barclays Capital U.S. Aggregate Bond Index are trademarks of Barclays Capital Inc. (Barclays Capital). NYSE Group, Inc. (NYSE:NYX) operates two securities exchanges: the New York Stock Exchange (the "NYSE") and NYSE Arca (formerly known as the Archipelago Exchange, or ArcaEx, and the Pacific Exchange). NYSE Group is a leading provider of securities listing, trading and market data products and services. The New York Mercantile Exchange, Inc. (NYMEX) is the world's largest physical commodity futures exchange and the preeminent trading forum for energy and precious metals, with trading conducted through two divisions - the NYMEX Division, home to the energy, platinum, and palladium markets, and the COMEX Division, on which all other metals trade. All information is believed to be from reliable sources; however we make no representation as to its completeness or accuracy. All economic and performance data is historical and not indicative of future results. Market indices discussed are unmanaged. Investors cannot invest in unmanaged indices. The publisher is not engaged in rendering legal, accounting or other professional services. If other expert assistance is needed, the reader is advised to engage the services of a competent professional. Please consult your Financial Advisor for further information.

Video: Fixed Index Annuity Choices

Click & Watch this video to find out more...

Video URL: http://annuityguys.com/choosing-a-fixed-index-annuity

QR Code for smart phones:

Chapter 7:
MarketFree™ Life Immediate Annuities

"John, was ironing for our neighbors the income plan you had in mind when you said no to that life immediate annuity and invested our last dime in SWAMPS-R-US?"

"Money frees you from doing things you dislike. Since I dislike doing nearly everything, money is handy." - Groucho Marx

Case Study 6 -- Sarah

After much discussion and planning, Sarah decided she was all set to retire within the next month, taking into consideration that she had CDs maturing a few days before retirement.

Therefore, as planned, Sarah placed the entire amount of her CDs-- over $400,000--into a financial instrument that would provide her with a regular income stream. As a result, her income would now be high enough to allow her to continue on with additional IRA investments of approximately $200,000.

Sarah has no family to leave money to, and she likes security and income that she can count on. For these reasons, she was able to maximize her income since she was not at all concerned about leaving money to heirs. Plus, she loved the idea that her income would be reliable without regard to what age she might live to.

Living long lives ran strong in her family. Her grandmother had lived to be nearly one hundred years old, so she felt the immediate annuity could potentially work out in her favor knowing that her payouts were based on normal life expectancies. She also liked the idea of 3 percent annual increases contractually guaranteed to her.

In essence, Sarah was looking for a way to place part of her retirement savings into a low-risk option that would provide her with a regular stream of good income--and a MarketFree™ immediate annuity was just the ticket that Sarah was looking for. This vehicle allowed her to make a lump sum premium allocation into an annuity, and almost immediately after making that deposit, Sarah was provided with a regular, reliable, and safe stream of retirement income that would last for the rest of her anticipated long life.

Understanding Life Immediate Annuities

Today, people are living longer than ever before. While the idea of living a longer (and hopefully healthier) life is appealing to most of us, the tradeoff for many people is the fear of outliving retirement savings.

On top of that, the immense costs of healthcare today--along with constantly rising inflation--continue to compound an already stressful situation for many. However, there is an option available to retirees that can help ease the stress of outliving savings while providing an income stream almost immediately after setting it up. That financial vehicle is called a life immediate annuity.

While many annuities are created to build up the account value for retirement, an immediate annuity is actually designed to provide income immediately to its owner/annuitant. Immediate annuities are insurance products that pay owners a regular income--monthly, quarterly, or over another desired time frame--for as long as the owner/annuitant lives.

These products are essentially a contract between the annuity owner and an insurance company. They are typically purchased with a large cash lump sum by retirees in order to pay living expenses with a reliable "pension style income" over a long period of time. In exchange for this lump sum deposit, the insurance company will provide the annuity owner/annuitant with a regular income for life, regardless of how long that may be. In Sarah's case, the insurance company may have a statistical anomaly costing them dearly! Go Girl!!!

An immediate annuity can almost be considered as the opposite of life insurance. Why is this? For one thing, life insurance provides a cash payment benefit to beneficiaries upon the insured's death. While an immediate annuity offers a cash benefit to the owner/annuitant while living.

Plus, if it is a lifetime annuity, this benefit will continue for as long as the owner/annuitant lives. And yes, it is possible for the immediate annuity owner's heirs to receive some of the intended income should the owner/annuitant die prematurely.

Fact or Fiction...Know the Truth!

Over the years, there have been almost as many myths as there are facts swirling around about immediate annuities. Let's dispel at least some of those un-truths.

Fact or Fiction: The greatest concern of retirees is the safety of his or her money. — Fiction!

While safety is definitely a concern, the greater concern of many retirees is outliving their money especially since life expectancy has increased dramatically. This is statistically a valid and important concern for the majority of retirees that strive to save enough money to provide an income that cannot be outlived. Immediate annuities, however, can help to solve this issue.

Fact or Fiction: If someone dies while owning an annuity, the insurance company always keeps all of the money. — Fiction!

The only time that this is true is in the case of a maximum income--life-only immediate annuity, other lesser income payout options on immediate annuities can leave money to heirs. Otherwise, most other types of annuities pay any un-spent account value to the beneficiaries of the annuity owner.

Fact or Fiction: Stocks or mutual funds will always outperform MarketFree™ immediate annuity payouts as a source of retirement income. — Fiction!

While stocks and mutual funds might potentially outperform the immediate annuity income, there is a definite risk and reward trade-off when owning stocks or mutual funds as compared to an immediate annuities contractual performance guarantees.

For example, if a mutual fund will be used to provide income, then there are certain investments and longevity risks that must be accepted which includes running out of money. In addition, the big issue of the retiree's risk of actually running out of money is possibly the fair trade-off to the reward of potentially higher income payments in the future.

Fact or Fiction: All future guaranteed annuity income payments will be lessened by inflation. — Fiction!

Immediate annuities can actually be obtained with an annual cost of living adjustment or COLA. This means that in many cases, the income payment can be increased by as much as 3 to 5 percent--possibly even more, based on a guaranteed rate or a consumer price index--annually.

Immediate Annuity Options

Traditional immediate annuities offer a fixed periodic payment in exchange for an initial lump sum of cash known as a premium. This type of annuity typically will not allow future access to the initial cash paid into the premium funding the immediate annuity. In essence, the cash asset or lump sum allocated to the immediate annuity is forfeited and is no longer accessible in its entirety. It is instead converted to a guaranteed income stream.

Throughout the years, there have been some modifications to the original immediate annuity design. Many of these annuity features - which may or may not be available on all immediate annuities or offered by all insurance companies, are discussed below:

Inflation Protection: With this feature, the immediate annuity income payments offer some form of a hedge against inflation. Here, the annuity owner may choose to have his or her income payments increase by a certain percentage each year, typically around 3 percent. Another choice may be to have the annuity income payments actually tied to an inflation measure by the use of a consumer price index. When either of these options are chosen, the initial payout of the annuity usually starts at a lower income level.

There are several different ways to structure an immediate annuity with regard to the income payment options. These options include:

Refund, Installment, & Period Certain Death Benefit Options: The refund option on immediate annuities has typically been either a cash refund or an installment refund, ensuring that at the annuity owners/annuitants pre-mature death the beneficiary will receive an amount of money that represents the difference between the initial premium and the amount of the income payments that the annuitant received during his or her life. These options, however, reduce the amount of the systematic income payout when comparing to life only with no beneficiary benefits.

Variable payments: With variable immediate annuities, the annuitant is allowed to direct the initial allocation into various investment options such as mutual funds - aka--sub-accounts. Therefore, depending upon the investment performance of the sub-accounts, the annuitant's periodic annuity income payments could certainly go up or down.

Life only: A life-only immediate annuity can also be referred to as a straight life annuity. This means that the annuitant will receive the highest allowable annuity income payments based on his or her average life expectancy, regardless of how long that duration may be. At death payments will cease and all of the initial premium will be to the insurance company's benefit or detriment based upon the annuitant's actual date of death based on the life expectancy underwriting calculations.

Certain period: This structure is not considered to be a life annuity. Rather, the annuity payments will only go on for a fixed or certain period of time, such as five, ten, or fifteen years. Even if the annuitant is still living at the end of the stated time period, the annuity payments will cease at that time. However, should annuitant pass away within that time period, income payments will continue to be paid to beneficiary(s) until the period of time ends.

Life with period certain (or certain and life): This immediate annuity payment option structure is a combination of both the life and the certain period structures – meaning, the annuity will pay income benefits to the annuitant for life with a smaller income amount than straight life only. However, if the annuitant passes away before the end a specified period of time, of say ten years, then the beneficiary(s) will continue to receive income payments from the annuity until the end of that ten-year time period.

Life with cash refund: This can be considered a money-back guarantee annuity. The income benefit payout is for life. If the annuitant passes away before all initial premium has been paid-out, the total amount of payments paid to the annuity owner will then be subtracted from the initial premium paid and the balance will be paid to the annuitant's beneficiary(s) in a lump sum payment.

Life with installment refund: This, too, can be considered a money-back guarantee annuity. This immediate annuity payout option is similar to the life with cash refund option, except that the annuitant's beneficiary(s) will continue to receive the monthly annuity income instead of a lump sum until the full amount of the premium has been paid back.

Joint and Survivor: This annuity income payout option will guarantee that the income payments will continue for the lives of both annuitants. Along with this, period certain options can also be added. This particular payout option is mainly used with married couples in order to provide income as long as either one is still alive.

COLA SPIA: This annuity income payout structure has payments that increase or decrease by a floating percentage which fluctuates when tied to a consumer price index each year. In this case, however, the initial income benefit will likely be lower compared to those which are non-COLA (cost of living adjustment) annuities.

Other Types of Immediate Annuities

There are some types of immediate annuities that may be set up for various specific reasons in order to meet certain needs of the owner/annuitant. Some of these include:

Medicaid Exempt Immediate Annuity

In some circumstances, the purchase of an immediate annuity can help to qualify for Medicaid assistance sooner, while still allowing individuals to potentially pass on a larger amount of estate assets to heirs. Essentially, the assets that are placed in a Medicaid exempt immediate annuity are no longer considered to be in the estate, but rather are considered as being "spent down" prior to Medicaid eligibility acceptance. States have varying standards that must be met for this type of annuity to be exempted.

Laddered Annuity Strategy

Using a laddered annuity strategy can actually provide income for a certain period of years from an immediate annuity, typically between five and ten. Simultaneously deferred annuities or other investments are used with the objective of earning back the original amount of the principal or more than what was allocated to the immediate annuity during the years it was depleted. This method is also used for foundational income planning with the new generation of income riders to reach an inflation hedged guaranteed income level for cash flow needs instead of just focusing on cash growth.

Some retirees have CDs from which interest is withdrawn each month or annually--with today's low rate environment it becomes increasingly difficult to avoid depleting principal. Many in retirement would like to leave the principal they started with to heirs while taking a generous income in retirement. By using a split or laddered annuity strategy, retirees may be able to increase the amount of income received while also having a guarantee of principal at the end of a specific time period.

This is a great concept, in that most of the income received from the immediate annuity may be received tax-exempt based on the exclusion ratio, and the deferred annuity's growth side is helped by the fact that it has tax-deferred growth and certain income guarantees. Now combining this with a Roth carve-out annuity can create an annuity portfolio on tax-free growth steroids.

Use of qualified experts is the key when it comes to utilizing these more advanced annuity strategies. This is where an advanced annuity specialist can make a dramatic improvement over the typical annuity salesperson. It is also important to note that there are typically no additional costs when choosing to work an advanced insurance licensed annuity specialist, so, choose to work with the best!

Immediate Annuity Benefits

There are numerous benefits to owning an immediate annuity. Some are similar to those of other types of annuities; however, an immediate annuity gives the added benefit of being able to receive a potentially larger income stream almost immediately following the premium payment or lump sum of principal used to purchase the annuity contract. Some of the primary benefits of an immediate annuity are:

Regular income stream immediately: An immediate annuity is a great source for receiving a regular stream of income. This is great for retirees. Having an immediate annuity allows one to receive a check of a certain amount on a set date and at regular intervals, and that income can begin as soon as one month but no later than twelve months following insurer's receipt of an immediate annuity premium. This is extremely helpful in planning a secure cash flow for retirement.

Protection from creditors: Many states allow creditor protection for annuity income to protect from litigation and creditors. Therefore, an immediate annuity can even be a good option if one was to face unfortunate circumstances and even bankruptcy. Fixed immediate annuities can also provide income during financial hardship in other areas of the economy regardless of market conditions.

Protection from a long term care Medicaid spend down: In addition to being protected from creditors-- annuity income can also be protected from Medicaid's forced spend down rules. In fact, using immediate annuities to shelter assets has actually become a type of long-term care planning technique for some (this has been somewhat controversial from an ethical point of view). However, by funding an immediate annuity, it is technically removing the funds from an estate (which helps with Medicaid qualification for long term care). Therefore, it is possible to meet the minimal asset requirements necessary in qualifying for long-term care benefits from Medicaid.

Fair Returns based on Life Expectancy: At times when interest rates are spiraling downward and income from other fixed-deposit instruments are shrinking, an immediate annuity could still offer an attractive rate of return. Living longer than actuarial life expectancy also increases returns substantially.

Exclusion ratio: The exclusion ratio refers to the amount of the annuity income that is not taxed, as it is deemed a repayment of the principal. Therefore, only the amount that is considered to be interest is taxed. In comparison, qualified funds such as those in IRAs and 401(K)'s are generally considered 100 percent taxable because in most cases the money in these accounts represents pre-tax dollars.

Immediate Annuity Performance

An immediate annuity's performance is dependent upon several factors. When setting up an immediate annuity for payout, the annuity owner controls the term and can choose from several options in receiving income including lifetime income, joint lifetime income, or simply the guarantee of income for a certain number of years.

The size of the monthly payment from an annuity will be based on some factors that are determined by the annuity provider such as the following:

- The amount allocated to the annuity contract, also referred to as the annuity premium;
- Whether one has chosen a fixed or a variable immediate annuity;
- The owner's age and life expectancy as well as the age and life expectancy of another person or spouse if a joint and survivor payout option is chosen;
- Medically rated immediate annuities are also available with larger payouts based on adverse health, potentially lowering life expectancy thus increasing income inversely.

Although the performance and the ultimate return of the immediate annuity may not offer the potential that stocks and mutual funds can offer, retirees will have the ultimate trade-off of receiving a guaranteed income that cannot be outlived without any danger of market risk wiping out one's life savings.

Most other types of financial vehicles simply cannot provide that option. Should an immediate annuity owner live longer than expected, his or her return increases dramatically; and the tables are turned from the insurance company to the owner/annuitants favor.

Immediate Annuity Disadvantages

Even with all of the advantages of immediate annuities, there are a few things that buyers need to be aware of prior to opting for this type of retirement income product.

Certainly, these annuities are not for everyone. Opting for an immediate annuity is a permanent decision that can essentially last for the remainder of a lifetime, so one needs to know all of the ins and outs of the product. Some of the drawbacks to consider with immediate annuities are outlined below.

Return: Although immediate annuities do offer a reliable and regular income stream, they are not purchased for their high returns. Immediate annuity owners can generally expect to receive conservative returns which will not be likely to exceed returns that can be found in the securities market, unless one lives longer than expected. (Hmm, why not?) However, the good news is that retirees will receive these returns and income with considerably more security.

Potential loss of purchasing power: It is a fact that since the amount of income will remain the same (in a fixed immediate level annuity without a COLA) this can actually be seen as a double-edged sword. While the regular stream of income is often seen as very secure for the owner/annuitant, there is the downside of the potential loss of purchasing power due to inflation.

Loss of a cash asset to purchase an immediate annuity: This, too, can be considered either a pro or con; depending upon the immediate annuity owners overall situation and the income payout option that is chosen. For instance, if the option selected is for the life income option on an immediate annuity, the income will be received for the rest of one's life. Should retiree live a longer life, this can work out very well making this a wise decision. If, however, the retiree should pass away soon after starting the annuity payout phase, then the insurance company will be able to keep the remainder of the un-paid out premium. This could be a big drawback to heirs who may not be happy with losing those funds for future needs. Therefore, one should be careful in choosing an income option that works best in light of one's overall financial situation, both now and in the future.

Irrevocable contracts: In general, immediate annuities are considered to be irrevocable contracts. So, once they have been funded as an annuity allocation, then liquidity is forever forfeited on the lump-sum used to fund the immediate annuity (other than systematic income or a refund during the annuity's "free look" period). The funds deposited into the annuity are considered non-refundable. Therefore, if more liquidity may be necessary or there is uncertainty about needing access to account balance in the future, then an immediate annuity may not be the best choice.

Choosing a Immediate Annuity

As individuals enter into retirement, income needs are often lower as compared to pre-retirement. Hence, spending needs typically decrease by 20-30 percent based on available statistics. It is important to be able to match the income need with the retirement dollars that are available to create an income stream. The financial vehicles that are chosen to generate that income will make a big difference as to the amount of income that will be received and for how long.

When considering an immediate annuity, one of the major factors affecting the income payment amount is life expectancy. The older the person, the shorter the life expectancy is. As a result, the income payment will be larger when it starts.

In addition, payments will also be based on current interest rates. So, depending upon the future outlook of the financial markets and the movements of interest rates, one should decide as to whether it is a good idea to begin annuity payments soon or just wait hoping for interest rates to rise.

In any case, depending upon each investors specific financial situation and goals, an immediate annuity could be a great choice for an individual or a couple in a joint survivor situation. For certain retirees whom are seeking a secure income right away--an immediate annuity is a highly tax-favored way of obtaining a guaranteed amount of income that one cannot outlive while avoiding riskier market-oriented investments.

Video: New Immediate Hybrid Annuities

Click & Watch this video to learn more...

Video URL: http://annuityguys.com/the-new-immediate-hybrid-annuity

QR Code for smart phones:

Chapter 8: MarketFree™ Hybrid Annuities

"Joe, I been a thinkin' and retirin' without income ain't the best ever ider ever. Ya reckon we might could start some kinda hybrid income retirement planin?"

"Inflation is when you pay fifteen dollars for the ten-dollar haircut you used to get for five dollars when you had hair."

-Sam Ewing

Case Study 7 -- Bob

At age sixty, Bob was in a real quandary as to what he should do with his retirement savings. Although considered young by retirement standards, Bob had reached a point in his life where he felt comfortable leaving the rat race within the next five years and living off his investable assets for the remainder of his life.

The "problem," however, came in the fact that Bob was healthy and active and could essentially live in retirement for another thirty plus years. So, Bob was struggling with how to achieve a lifetime retirement income while still allowing his money to keep pace with inflation over the next few decades.

As Bob discussed the situation, he looked at securities, bank instruments, and various annuities. He was pleased to discover that there was a hybrid annuity solution available that would allow him to not only receive a guaranteed amount of lifetime income but also allow his funds to take part in market gains--all while eliminating the investment risk he was trying to avoid in retirement!

Bob was relieved that he could allocate a portion of his portfolio, approximately $950,000 from his assets of about $2 million, for a retirement income foundation in his portfolio. Bob diversified by using four different insurers, one for a five year immediate annuity and the other three offering hybrid style fixed index annuities which would also include income riders that are frequently referred to as living benefits. The hybrid annuities could actually guarantee Bob an annual rate for income growth (known as an income floor) to hedge against inflation, regardless of how the market performed. In addition, Bob could also have a death benefit available to him that could be structured to allow him the potential that his heirs would receive back his original principal or more when Bob passes away.

Bob now feels more comfortable investing some of his portfolio more aggressively since he has the retirement income foundation secure and growing. Bob laddered his MarketFree™ hybrid annuities and he plans to turn income on at five year intervals to hedge against inflation.

Understanding Hybrid Annuities

MarketFree™ Hybrid annuities, also referred to as hybrid income annuities, are essentially a type of insurance contract with a linked market benchmark component--having an income rider and/or other riders that give substantial present or future guarantees in securing a variety of retirement objectives.

These annuities have a combination of several unique aspects of various types of annuities that have been combined. Technically, a hybrid annuity is a fixed annuity having an index option with an innovative new generation income rider.

Some hybrid annuities can help to resolve the concerns with other needs in addition to asset growth and retirement income--such as long-term care funding or wealth transfer to heirs--while still providing one with a secure income. These annuities are considered by many to be the answer to satisfying a combination of retirement objectives, thus having the potential of solving several retirement issues with one financial instrument.

Obtaining a hybrid annuity essentially works the same way as one chooses any annuity. Ones allocation to hybrid annuity begins by choosing the hybrid annuity--after comparing rates, features and ratings that meet key retirement objectives.

With some hybrids, if funds are required for needs such as long-term care, owners can have access to withdrawals for that purpose by way of an accelerated cash account payout or a guaranteed increased income payout with no penalty for as long as it is needed. However, if one does not need funds for long term care, the owner/annuitant will receive the lifetime guaranteed retirement income just as it was structured, or use the annuity for moderate growth allocation as a safe asset foundation to a balance portfolio.

Fact or Fiction... Know the Truth!

As MarketFree™ hybrid annuities are not an actual specific annuity (hybrid actually describes the combination of benefits offered by various types of different annuities combined into one). There are many misconceptions with regard to how these annuities work as well as how the benefits are received. Therefore, it is important to fully understand what fact is and what fiction is when it comes to hybrid annuities or hybrid income annuities.

Fact or Fiction: If retirees use some of their annuity account value, then eligibility is lost to receive any long-term care benefit dollars. — Fiction!

The truth is that on certain hybrid types--even if retirees use all of the account value for guaranteed retirement income needs--if one opted for the additional long-term care or income rider, then the owner will still be able to receive a certain dollar amount for a long-term care need as well. This essentially can be an answer that gives retirees the best of both worlds; guaranteed income and a long-term care payout that's guaranteed.

Fact or Fiction: If one dies before using the hybrid annuity income, there will be nothing left for heirs. — Fiction!

Unlike immediate annuities or annuitization which is allowed on all annuities, with a hybrid annuity, the heirs typically will receive all of the remaining dollars including any bonus with no penalties or surrender charges should the owner/annuitant pass away prior to spending the annuities cash value.

This can be extremely comforting for many who want children or other heirs to receive a substantial inheritance, yet also need the benefit of guaranteed retirement income and access to account value for unexpected expenses.

Fact or Fiction: Because of the market indexing component, hybrid annuities are risky. — Fiction!

The facts are that hybrid index annuities offer interest crediting that is linked to the upside growth of popular stock indexes, without the downside risks of any loss from down markets. In addition, index annuities are technically just fixed annuities that are principal protected as guaranteed assets by the claims paying ability of highly rated insurance companies, and can be used as part of a predictable and comprehensive financial plan.

They are also excellent retirement and estate planning financial tools due to the fact that they are built with contractual guarantees. These types of annuities are quite suitable for funds that should not be put at risk of market loss they should be used as a safe retirement allocation in a well balanced portfolio.

Fact or Fiction: MarketFree™ Hybrid annuities have high fees like variable annuities. — Fiction!

No fees or low fees is one of the great advantages of hybrid annuities; other than the income rider fee or a spread of typically less than 1 percent (income riders are mostly optional). A spread simply means that if there is no gain, there is no fee.

Fact or Fiction: Hybrid annuities protect principal and lock in earnings. — Fact!

Never going backward with principal or earnings is a benefit that makes hybrid annuities so popular--this allows a safe Gain and Retain strategy. The chassis for a hybrid annuity is actually a fixed annuity with a market indexing option, also known as a fixed index annuity (FIA).

Fact or Fiction: Hybrid annuities give the full upside of a popular market index with no downside risk — Fiction!

Unfortunately, overzealous insurance/annuity salespeople have misrepresented hybrid annuities as getting the full upside of the market. It is true; however, hybrid annuities have no downside risk. Also, these annuities have caps, averaging spreads, and participation rates that limit upside gain in return for no downside risk. Ironically, this does allow hybrid and other fixed annuities with indexing options to do better than the market indices they are linked to when market conditions are volatile, flat, or down over a period of years.

Hybrid Annuity Features

Some common retirement concerns that are frequently articulated are as follows:

- The need for reliable income now or in the future;
- Maintain financial independence;

- To know that cash will never run out;
- Guarantee income for a surviving spouse;
- Guarantee income and still leave money to heirs;
- Avoid long-term care asset spend-down;
- Have an inflation hedge without market risk.

Hybrid annuities are not a panacea or silver bullet; however, they can help overcome specific retirement concerns by combining the benefits of various financial products and different annuities into one. And since hybrid annuities consist of a fixed index annuity combined with an innovative income rider, let's see how this unique combination of annuity benefits answers each of the retirement concerns enumerated above.

For openers, income can be started immediately with an inflation-hedged option or deferred with guaranteed growth of the income account at 6 to 10 percent compounded or simple interest calculation. As a result, future income also has a guaranteed increase to battle inflation. With income payout options; single or joint, the income is guaranteed for life. This secures financial independence of the annuity owner/annuitant and/or that of a spouse.

When living beyond a normal life expectancy, it is possible to run out of cash account value but never run out of income on a lifetime payout. As long as the owner/annuitant is living, income continues. Hybrid annuity owners remain in majority control of the cash asset used to fund the hybrid income annuity. From day one, the owner exercises majority control over the full account value. This allows an owner can reclaim approximately 90 percent of what was initially allocated in premium, and every year for approximately ten years, the majority control increases until eventually the owner(s) is back to 100 percent control.

In addition, from day one, all 100 percent of the cash account value that has not been used for income will go to heirs, including earnings, if any, or bonus in the account. Children/heirs will typically receive the full unused account value with no penalties or surrenders.

Long-term care and lifetime income provisions built into hybrid annuities or achieved with optional riders vary in design. Some are a more complete answer, and some help supplement a potential extended care need.

Also, all of this is accomplished with guarantees, avoiding any and all market risk.

As one may be aware that the indexing portion of the hybrid income annuity uses a linked market index--offering potential market upside with absolutely no downside market risk, in addition it can also create a lifetime income while simultaneously allowing majority control of the account value and supplement a long term care need too! So, this essentially creates a unique win-win-win situation.

So how do these hybrid annuities work for long-term care? Although there are many differences in the hybrid annuities, the basic premise is that the contract allows for growth on one's money while providing a long term care solution with an easier way to qualify for a long-term care benefit. The hybrid chassis is a fixed index annuity, in that it will provide safety, growth, and a lifetime of income. In addition to that, there may be a long-term care option available as a separately purchased rider or included at no additional cost with the income rider.

In some cases, the long-term care rider on the account means that the purchase will require some form of medical underwriting for approval. This may entail a health questionnaire and possibly a physical examination.

Once approved (only if required), and if long-term care services are needed in the future, initially a portion of the cash account value from the hybrid annuity may be used to pay for those long-term care needs. The long-term care coverage in some hybrid income annuities may be determined based on the amount of coverage that is selected when making application for a hybrid annuity.

Depending on the issuing insurance company, the company may offer a payout of between two and three times the initial policies account value, typically paid out over two to four additional years after the annuity cash account value is depleted.

As an example, if one were to deposit $100,000 into hybrid annuity and selected a benefit limit of 300 percent and a four-year long-term care benefit rider, then one would essentially have an additional $200,000 over and above the initial $100,000 deposit that could be used for long-term care expenses (even after the initial $100,000 of annuity policy value was depleted). So in other words, for $100,000 premium, one could actually end up with a potential payout for long-term care expenses of $300,000--if structured correctly this can also be a tax free benefit.

Another method is referred to as a Long Term Care Doubler or a Home Health Care Doubler which essentially allows the lifetime guaranteed income to be doubled for a limited time such as five years. With some annuities the doubler is unlimited for the entire duration of the long term care stay.

In addition, due to the Pension Protection Act of 2006 that became effective in January 2010, an annuity owner may receive some of these long-term care benefits from this type of annuity on a tax-free basis. This offers considerably more value than if taxes were due on these long term care distributions.

Hybrid Annuity Benefits

Some of the numerous benefits associated with owning a hybrid annuity include:

- Flexibility in design during the initial set up;
- Accelerated (typically 5%-8%) growth of the income account in deferral to maximize future lifetime income payouts;
- Potential inflation hedge of annually increasing income;
- Upside market potential via the use of indices such as the Dow Jones or the S&P 500;
- Essentially no actual stock market investment with no downside market risk;
- An income rider option that guarantees contractual lifetime income for a single or joint payout;
- An income that cannot be outlived;
- Typically, 10 percent annual penalty-free withdrawals

- Majority control of approximately 90% of the full account value (of an income producing asset) with a declining surrender charge bringing 100% control typically over a ten-year period of time;

- The ability to leave to heirs, as an inheritance, the full cash value of an annuity balance that has not been fully depleted by long term income withdrawals;
- Long-term care benefits.

Index Riders & Contractual Guarantees

"Absolute guarantees -- No-moving parts."

Hybrid-/Fixed Index-Annuities--allow for upside potential while having specific moving parts in addition to absolute contractual guarantees.

Income Rider - addendum to a hybrid index annuity contract, guaranteeing a future lifetime income plus additional specified benefits in some income riders (this is an absolute contractual guarantee).

Hybrid Annuity Specifics

1. Annuity Owner Remains in majority control of the annuity's cash account value during the surrender term and has 100% control after the surrender term at maturity.

2. Full account value of the cash account passes on to heirs with no surrender or penalty charge.

3. Guaranteed growth for income in deferral guaranteeing a minimum future income.

Example: Initial Premium $100,000 + 5% bonus guaranteed growth of 7.2 percent deferred for ten years = $210,000 income account value producing a guaranteed income of $12,600 per year at age 70 with a single life payout.

4. Payout percentages from the income account are based on age and a single or joint income need.

Example: Age seventy - single payout, 6 percent or joint payout, 5.5 percent

5. Fees for riders can be based on the cash or income account value and are paid out of the cash account. Fees typically range from half of one percent (.5%) to one and a quarter percent (1.25%). This does not reduce the

guaranteed growth of the income account also referred to as an annual rollup or income floor.

6. May have a death benefit allowing the income account, if it is larger than the cash account, to be distributed to heirs over a five-year period.

7. May have an increasing income as an inflation hedge.

8. May have a Long Term Care Benefit.

Hybrid Index Strategy Moving Parts

Index examples: *S&P 500, *Dow Jones Industrial, *Trader Vic -- (*Commodities Strategy),

Uncapped Index - the full percentage of earnings growth on an index to be applied as interest to the cash account value and income account value if it exceeds the contractually guaranteed growth.

Cap - limits the percentage of earnings growth on an index to be applied as interest to the cash account value and income account value.

•**Positive Example:** 3% Cap *S&P index is up 10% for the year; interest credited is 3%.

•**Negative Example:** 3 % Cap *S&P index is down 10% for the year; interest credited is 0%.

Spread - a fee based on a percentage subtracted first, only when index earnings exist. Any earnings are applied as interest to the cash account value and income account value. If there are no earnings, the spread is never applied.

•**Positive Example:** 3% Spread *S&P index is up 10% for the year; interest credited is 7%.

•**Negative Example:** 3% Spread *S&P index is down 10% for the year; interest credited is 0%; the spread is no longer applicable.

Participation - allows a percentage of index growth to be applied as interest to the cash account value and income account value.

- **Positive Example:** 30% Participation *S&P index is up 10% for the year; interest credited is 3%.

- **Negative Example:** 30% Participation *S&P index is down 10% for the year; interest credited is 0%.

Average - allows the average index growth to be applied as interest to the cash account value and income account value over a specified period of time.

- **Positive Example:** *S&P index is at 100 at the beginning of the year and it fluctuates up and down - between 110 and 100 for the year, with six months of the index being at 110 and six months at 100. The average annual interest credited is 5%.

- **Formula:** (110+100+110+100+110+100+110+100+110+100+110+100)
$$=1260/12=105-100 = 5\%$$

- **Negative Example:** *S&P index is at 100 at the beginning of the year and it fluctuates up and down - between 100 and 90 for the year, with six months of the index being at 100 and six months at 90. The average annual interest credited is 0%.

- **Formula:** (90+100+90+100+90+100+90+100+90+100+90+100)
$$=1140/12=95-100 = -5\%$$

Capped Monthly Sum or Average - allows for adding together each months index growth limited by a cap to the upside with no cap limit to the downside in any month. The downside is subtracted from the cumulative total. Cumulative earnings are applied as interest to the cash account value and income account value over a specified period of time.

- **Positive Example:** *S&P index is up 12% for the year, however; six months were 0% earnings and six months were 2% earnings each. The monthly cap is 1%, the annual interest credited is 6%.

- **Formula:** (0% x 6 months = 0%) + (1% x 6 months = 6%) = 6%

- **Negative Example:** *S&P index is up 12% for the year, however; six months were negative 2% earnings and six months were 4% earnings each. The monthly cap is 1%. The annual interest credited is 0%.

- **Formula:** (-2% x 6 months = -12%) + (1% x 6 months = 6%) = -6%

Blend - combining a specified percentage of account value to an uncapped index for earnings growth with a specified percentage of account value based on a fixed interest portion. Then add all gains and any losses to determine the interest to be applied to the cash account value and income account value.

•**Positive Example:** *S&P index is up 10% for the year; 50% of the blend is an uncapped index and 50% of the blend is a fixed rate of 2%. The annual interest credited is 6%.

•**Formula:** (10% x 50% = 5%) + (2% x 50%= 1%) = 6%

•**Negative Example:** *S&P index is down 10% for the year; 50% of the blend is an uncapped index and 50% of the blend is a fixed rate of 2%. The annual interest credited is 0%.

•**Formula:** (-10% x 50% = -5%) + (2% x 50%= 1%) = -4%

Fees - are typically associated with optional riders. Fees are subtracted from cash value accounts, not affecting income guarantee accounts. Fees may reduce principal in years with no interest earnings. (Some rider fees are specified as a spread and do not lower cash account value in years with no interest earnings).

Index Strategies & Various Time Periods...

with combinations of the components described above:

- Annual Point-to-Point with a Cap
- Annual Point-to-Point Average with a Spread
- Annual Point-to-Point Capped Monthly Average or Monthly Sum
- Point-to-Point with a Participation Rate
- Biennial Point-to-Point with a Biennial Cap
- Quadrennial Point-to-Point with a Quadrennial Blend
- Five Year Point to Point with an Uncapped Non-Correlated Commodity Index

Choosing a Hybrid Annuity

There are multiple features available with hybrid annuities that can greatly enhance income and financial security in retirement. And with longer life expectancies today, a guarantee of a lifetime income available thru options of –single or joint-, along with the added benefit of an inflation hedge and payment for potential long-term care expenses, hybrid annuities provide a retirement solution to meet multiple retirement needs. Below is a review of what hybrid income annuities have the potential to solve:

- The need for reliable income now or in the future;
- Maintain financial independence;
- Know that cash for income will never run out;
- Guarantee income for a surviving spouse;
- Guarantee income and still leave money to heirs;
- Avoid long-term care asset spend-down;
- Have an inflation hedge without market risk.

Hybrid Annuity Disadvantages

Although hybrid annuities can seem to give the best of many worlds, there are some things that one needs to be aware of prior to choosing a hybrid annuity for retirement income. These factors include:

- Cash account value may have a low annual percentage yield, 2%-4%;
- Many hybrid annuities do not have increasing income as an inflation hedge, as this is only used on more specific and unique hybrid annuities;
- The upside market potential using linked market indices could be limited by poor market performance;
- There are some fees involved for the income riders;
- Making any excessive withdrawals in the early years of the account may have a surrender charge;
- Heirs may be responsible for paying income tax on what is inherited, depending upon how the annuity was structured;
- Not all hybrid-style annuities offer a long-term care benefit;

- Once the annuity leaves the deferral stage to begin the income stage, the higher roll-up growth in the income account typically ends.

Video: MarketFree™ Hybrid Annuities

Click & Watch this video to find out more...

Video URL: http://annuityguys.com/what-are-marketfree-hybrid-annuities

QR Code for smart phones:

Chapter 9: Annuity Riders

"Now, Helen, are you sure he said this rider guarantees unlimited marital bliss? Or does that fall under our unlimited strong prescription drug provision?"

"When I was young, I used to think that money was the most important thing in life... and now that I am old, I know it is."

-Oscar Wilde

Case Study 8 -- Teresa and Ann

When Teresa, Ann's mother, was sixty years old, she had put $100,000 into an annuity. For twenty years, Teresa allowed the funds to grow and by the time she turned eighty, her health had already deteriorated appreciably after being diagnosed with Alzheimer's a couple of years earlier. She was now to the point where her doctor strongly recommended that she receive full-time long-term care assistance.

Since Teresa did not own any long-term care insurance, her daughter, Ann, had little choice other than to recommend that she cash out the funds in her annuity which at approximately 4 percent growth had grown to $219,000. After paying approximately $36,000 in federal tax on the gain, Ann was left with $183,000 to help pay for her mother's care. Although this was a nice sum of money, Teresa's daughter feared that her mother could run out of funds quickly, depending upon how long she would require care.

However, if Teresa had acquired a long-term care benefit rider on her initial annuity purchase, the situation would be quite different. Long-term care riders allow an annuity owner to access funds with higher guarantees for qualifying long-term care needs tax free.

For instance, if Teresa had been able to choose a long-term care rider of the variety available today, one that paid out up to two or three times her annuity account value—assuming an additional annual fee for this rider of 65 basis points—then at age eighty, Teresa's annuity account value would have grown to $193,000. While this amount is less than in the previous scenario, because of this rider, she would actually have had access to about $385,000 to $579,000 (the differing amounts depend upon the rider chosen) in tax-free dollars to be used over time for her long-term care needs, making a substantial difference for her financial well being--helping to pay for her continued specialized care.

Understanding Annuity Riders

A rider is a provision in an insurance contract or annuity policy that allows for additional benefits added to its terms or coverage. Riders are not automatically included or available in all policies, but for those riders that are available, the policy or annuity holder will sometimes be charged an extra fee for choosing the rider.

Before finalizing an annuity contract, it is important to understand annuity riders and whether *a death benefit rider, a living benefit rider, an increasing payment option rider, a long-term care rider, or another type of rider* is available and then determine if it is suitable or necessary for one's specific situation.

Death Benefit Riders

Some annuities include a rider that acts like a life insurance benefit. If the annuity owner passes away before collecting the full value of the annuity, then the rider will pay the heirs the amount that the annuity owner had invested plus some predetermined interest or earnings, or the market value of the annuity account value's balance minus whatever has already been paid out in distributions.

Variable annuities have typically offered a guaranteed death benefit during the accumulation phase. This guaranteed minimum death benefit can give the annuity owner more confidence to invest in the securities market, as well as the security to know that his or her family will at the least be protected against a financial loss of the initial principal invested if the annuity holder should pass away when the account value has dropped from investment loss.

With annuities, the death benefit going to heirs incur ordinary income tax rates. This tax status is different than the death benefit on a life insurance policy that passes to the heirs tax-free. Roth accounts can be set up as annuities or established Roth accounts can be rolled over into annuities to create a tax free death benefit or lifetime tax free income. This strategy is used by astute advisors that understand the power of tax free annuities structured optimally for savvy retirees who recognize and appreciate the power of safe tax free compounding over time.

The death benefit that is payable from an annuity will typically be the remaining account value as of the date of the annuity owner's death. With variable annuities, a standard death benefit is based on the higher sum of the account value or the original premium less any withdrawals. Some income riders on hybrid annuities also allow the higher of the income account value or the cash account value; however, the income account value must normally be taken over a five year period, when that option is available.

In other cases, an annuity may offer an enhanced guaranteed death benefit that is based on a specific rate of return, minus any withdrawals, that is not based on the amount that is present in the annuities account value at the time of death. There is typically an additional rider fee that is added in order to provide this type of guaranteed growth benefit.

In any case, an annuity death benefit is handled in a different manner from that of life insurance death benefit. Oftentimes, the tax treatment of death benefits depends upon who the beneficiary(s) is and the insurance company's payout options, in addition to the qualified tax status of the annuity.

For example, as long as the death benefit proceeds stay inside the annuity, then they will not be considered taxable. In certain cases, the surviving spouse of the annuity owner could be able to keep the annuity by way of spousal continuation then do a 1035 annuity exchange or for tax-qualified-annuities use the death benefit proceeds in a sixty day rollover to another tax qualified annuity or an IRA in his or her own name. The death benefit proceeds can then continue growing on a tax-deferred or even a tax-free basis if the annuity is a Roth account. The initial issuing insurance company also allows a non-spouse beneficiary or a surviving spouse the choice of receiving the death benefit directly, which will create a taxable event in most circumstances.

Should the annuity owners surviving spouse elect to receive the death benefit directly, then the surviving spouse will be required to pay income tax on the amount of the difference between the death benefit and the amount that was initially contributed to the annuity (less any withdrawals that were made from the account).

Should the situation be that the beneficiary of the annuity is not a surviving spouse, the earnings in the annuity's cash value or death benefit account could be considered taxable to the receiver of those funds at his or her ordinary tax rate. In addition, the value of the annuity will also be included in the annuity owner's estate for tax purposes, and estate taxes if eligible will also be due on that amount.

Typically, the recipient of the death benefit proceeds will also have the choice of receiving the funds in a lump sum or as payments over time. By spreading out the payments over time, the beneficiary(s) will also essentially spread out and lower his or her tax liability.

Types of Death Benefit Riders

There are several types of enhanced guaranteed minimum death benefit rider options available on the market today. These include:

Contract Anniversary Value or Ratchet

Some annuity issuers will offer a death benefit rider that allows the benefit to step up or increase based on predetermined criteria. These are often referred to as a contract anniversary value or a ratchet-style death benefit. These enhanced guaranteed minimum death benefits are equal to the greater of either the contract value at the annuity holder's death, the amount of premiums paid into the annuity minus any prior withdrawals, or the contract value on a specified prior date when the annuity had positive earnings.

This specified date could be the annuity anniversary date, or (for example)the date at the end of every three-, five-, or ten-year period, every annual anniversary date, or even more often depending on the issuers contract. A ratchet guaranteed minimum death benefit can lock in the contract's gains on each of the dates specified.

Initial Purchase Payment with Minimum Interest or Rising Floor

Some annuity issuers will offer a minimum rising floor guaranteed minimum death benefit that is equal to the greater of either the annuity account value at the owner's death or the amount of premiums paid minus any prior withdrawals at a predetermined minimum rate of interest. This type of death benefit is typically increased annually at a specified rate of interest.

While some annuity contracts offer a choice of either a ratchet or a rising floor, there are others that may offer both within the same annuity.

Enhanced Earnings Benefits

In some cases, variable annuity death benefits have more than basic death benefit principal protection against falling markets. For example, instead, some variable annuities offer enhanced earning guarantees as death benefits that can provide a higher death benefit in order to guarantee gains even when investment losses occur, and this can also be considered as an offset to help pay ordinary income tax that is payable upon death by beneficiaries on any realized gains in the annuity's value.

With this feature, the beneficiary will not only receive the base amount of the death benefit, but will also receive an additional amount that is equal to a pre-determined percentage of growth guaranteed by the contract's death benefit if it is larger than the earnings in the actual account value. These enhanced variable annuity benefits usually have a hefty price tag of 1 to 2 percent or more charged annually.

Living Benefit Riders

Living benefit riders are another optional rider benefit that may be chosen on many annuity contracts. These riders must be requested at the time an annuity owner purchases an annuity. It is normally not allowed to add a living benefit rider to an existing annuity.

The first income riders were introduced on variable annuities just prior to the turn of this century and were created to protect the annuities ability to generate future income--when investment risk to principal or an account value produces a loss. This is accomplished by guaranteeing the minimum level of income that can exceed what would be payable based on the annuity investment account value. If the investment account value is less, the income is paid at a higher income rate regardless of weak growth or losses in the variable annuity investment account value. These types of riders became competitively available on fixed, as well as fixed index or hybrid annuities a few years after they were introduced on variable annuities. So, not only can the income be guaranteed but also the principal since it is a fixed annuity which is by state regulation required to be contractually guaranteed while one is living.

These riders can provide annuity owner with a guaranteed income for life, and--unlike the immediate annuity--without the need to give up access to the annuities principal or account cash value.

A living benefit rider can help reduce the risk of substantial loss by providing guaranteed income payouts for the risk-averse variable annuity holder. Although these riders require additional fees, they will provide a secure guarantee to protect the variable annuity income against declines in the market, in addition to providing a guaranteed minimum income that will not fluctuate based on the underlying investments.

With income riders, the income value is totally separate from the annuity's accumulation value or cash account. Normally with variable annuities, this income value will grow at a 5 to 6 percent compounding interest rate. With hybrid or fixed index annuities, it typically has higher income account growth compounded at 6 to 8 percent. Then, when an annuity owner starts taking lifetime withdrawals from the account, there is a payout percentage factor (based on an owner or joint payee's age) that is applied to the income value in order to determine the amount of the guaranteed-for-life income withdrawals. For example; a seventy year old retiree may be allowed to take a 6 percent draw on his or her income account value of say one million dollars, which equates to sixty thousand dollars of income annually as long as the retiree is alive. This is true even if a seventy year old retiree's cash value account has only seven hundred thousand dollars, accumulated from low interest earnings and runs out in twelve- to fourteen-years or so with continued poor earnings.

If the cash accumulation value is higher than the income account value when the annuity owner starts receiving an annuity income, then the accumulation value will be used in the calculation of the life payout instead of the minimum guaranteed income account value. Once the guaranteed withdrawal payout percentage amount is determined based on age, the annuity owner may then begin to withdraw that amount of annuity income each year on a monthly, quarterly, semiannual, or annual basis throughout the remainder of the annuitants' life. When the annuity owner begins receiving the lifetime income payout, the annuity will typically have several guarantees.

Two of these include:

1. The crediting of interest earned to the annuity's cash account value, along with majority control for continued access to the cash account when or as needed from any remaining cash account balance. (Warning: withdrawals in excess of the income guarantees can substantially lower guaranteed income being paid out for life)
2. Even though the annual guaranteed withdrawals from the annuity may deplete the cash accumulation account value over time, the issuing insurance company must continue to make the guaranteed income payments as long as the annuity owner is living, including income to the spouse if a joint payee is selected.

Types of Living Benefit Riders

There are several types of living benefit riders, and they all differ in terms of the benefits that they can provide. Some terms and acronyms are used interchangeably with entirely different meanings, so it is important to define terms before jumping to wrong conclusions. Some of the riders available are the:

Guaranteed Minimum Income Benefit Rider, GMIB

This living benefit rider guarantees a minimum future income payout, regardless of how the market performs. However, this rider may require that the accumulation phase of the annuity be kept in force for a specified time period before the rider will take effect.

This rider is designed to provide the annuity owner/annuitant with a base amount of lifetime income when income is needed at a future date, regardless of how the interest or investments of the annuity may have underperformed.

It will guarantee that when the annuity owner is eligible to annuitize the contract--either for life, life plus a certain time period, or for the lives of two individuals--then the annuity income payments will be based on the greater of either the amount that was contributed plus earnings or a maximum prior account value (aka-high water mark) at a predetermined interest rate compounded prior to annuitization.

In order to receive this benefit, the annuity owner must annuitize the account. In addition, there is normally a required holding period of ten years before this rider may be exercised.

Guaranteed Minimum Accumulation Benefit Rider, GMAB

This living benefit rider will ensure that the annuity owner is able to retain the value of the contributions plus a minimum growth, regardless of potential investment losses or lower earnings. This benefit will also require a specified period of time to determine if the annuity's investments or interest comes in lower than the guarantee; the annuity issuer will then make up the difference in income, accumulation, or death benefit as required.

In other words, the guaranteed minimum accumulation benefit rider will guarantee that an annuity owner's income account value will be at least equal to a certain minimum percentage of the amount that was contributed after a specified number of years, regardless of the actual performance of the investments. Typically, the holding period is somewhere between five and ten years.

Guaranteed Minimum Withdrawal Benefit Rider, GMWB

This living benefit rider option will guarantee a return of the premium amount through a series of fixed annual withdrawals. These annual withdrawals are guaranteed until the annuity holder's principal is returned, regardless of the investment performance or interest earnings.

This rider guarantees that a certain percentage of the amount that is contributed can be withdrawn annually until the entire amount is completely recovered, regardless of market performance. It should be noted that reducing the amount of the withdrawal in one year may not allow the annuitant to increase withdrawals in subsequent years.

However, if the annuity owner decides to defer the withdrawals and the value of the annuity account grows, then the amount of subsequent withdrawals that are allowed could be larger.

In the case of variable annuity sub-accounts, if the investments perform well then there will be an excess amount in the account at the end of the withdrawal period. However, if the underlying investments perform poorly and the value of the annuity account is depleted before the end of the withdrawal period, then the annuity owner can still continue making withdrawals until the full amount of the original premium contributions are recovered.

Guaranteed Lifetime Withdrawal Benefit, GLWB

Another more recent type of guaranteed minimum withdrawal benefit that was introduced into the annuity rider family is the guaranteed lifetime withdrawal benefit. It guarantees that a certain percentage of the income account value--usually 4 to 8 percent for single life or reduced slightly for joint life based upon the youngest of the annuitant's or spouse's age--this income payout precentage may be withdrawn each year for as long as the annuity owner or spouse, if joint, lives.

While in deferral, this type of guaranteed lifetime withdrawal benefit can compound at 6 to 8 percent or more on a contractually guaranteed basis. This is not to be confused with the actual annuity cash value account. This account has no actual cash value. It is simply an accounting ledger used to determine minimum income owed at the present or some future date. As a rule, the compounding or simple interest contractual guarantee is based on all premium paid in with any bonus added, then compounded annually or simple interest added for a specified period of time.

Surrenders

Majority control, allows the owner of deferred annuities to surrender the contract and receive a cash payment at any time. The amount that is received is called the cash account value or cash surrender value. This sum is equal to the amount of premium paid into the annuity plus any earnings, minus any prior withdrawals and minus any surrender charges. In the first year this usually equates to about 90 percent of the premium returned based on a full surrender and at maturity of the annuity 100 percent would be retuned plus any bonus and earnings if applicable.

The annuity owner may also take a specified partial withdrawal--not fully surrendering the annuity during the accumulation phase without incurring a penalty. However, there may be some surrender penalties incurred if more than a typical 10 percent penalty-free portion is withdrawn, surrender penalties are usually about 10 percent of the initial premium annually in the first years and then declining in subsequent years. Note, federal income tax early withdrawal penalties may be also be levied on earnings when taken before the age of fifty-nine and a half.

When Are Living Benefits Riders Right?

To truly determine if a living benefit rider is best for a retirement plan, it is important to understand exactly what one's objectives are. For example, certain questions should be answered, such as:

- Does the annuity income stream need to start soon or at some future date?
- How much income will be needed?
- Is it important to leave money to heirs?
- Is long-term care spend-down a concern?
- How much control should be maintained over the money?
- Is outliving income a concern?

Once the answers to these questions about a retiree's specific situation are determined, there is more information that must be gathered about the income rider being considered.

Some of the important rider questions are:

What is the roll-up rate? Many annuity income benefit riders offer a guaranteed rate of growth, or roll-up, or minimum floor of between 5 to10 percent. This roll-up rate is the guaranteed annual rate at which the income base will grow. Therefore, if an annuity with a contribution amount of $100,000 plus a bonus offers a ten-year income rider with an 8 percent annual compounding roll-up, then the income base could be $215,892 at the end of ten years. Then, at the end of the ten years, the income stream from the annuity would be based on an annual percentage income payout of the income base determined by the annuitant's or joint payee's age (using the youngest age for joint to determine the payout percentage) at the time that the payout phase began.

Is the interest being credited compound or simple? When comparing different types of annuity income riders, it is important to truly understand the type of interest being credited. For example, a 10 percent roll-up rate is typically going to be based on simple interest, and 10 percent simple interest is the same as 7.2 percent compounded for ten years. After ten years the compounded rate grows much faster and larger.

How many years can the income base accumulate? There are many income riders that will not allow the income base to accumulate beyond ten years before the annuity owner must start taking the income payout. However, there are some that allow much longer accumulation periods.

What are the fees now, and can those fees increase over time? Many annuity income riders have current fees of between .40 percent and .95 percent. Some annuities may increase their income rider fees after a specified number of years, up to 1.5 percent or more.

What account are the fees paid from? It is important to understand that fees are being deducted from the cash account value even when the cash value does not grow. In this case, it would be better to have a spread than a fee, since spreads are only deducted from the cash value if gains exist.

When are fees or spreads deducted? Typically, fees will be deducted on a monthly basis. However, some annuity issuers will deduct them on an annual basis.

Will the income base on the annuity continue accumulating even if the annuity owner takes a free partial withdrawal or a required minimum distribution from the base contract? With some income riders, the income base account will stop the guaranteed roll-up percentage temporarily or even forever if a partial withdrawal is taken.

Are there any additional benefits triggered for long-term care or the loss of function in doing basic daily activities at home? Sometimes, an annuity will offer to increase or even double the income benefit in these types of cases.

Can the annuity owner remove the income benefit rider from the annuity? Some income benefit riders are revocable while others are not.

Is it possible to get more than just the accumulation value upon death? With most income riders, when the annuitant takes annuity income, it will deplete the accumulation. When the annuity owner/annuitant passes away, then heirs will not receive the income base account. Instead, heirs will receive whatever amount is left of the accumulation account value; if the annuitant lives a long life, there may not be anything left. There are a few annuities that allow the income base, if it is greater than the accumulation account, to be paid out to heirs over a specified period of time typically five years.

Long-Term Care Rider

Some annuities offer features that are designed to address long-term care needs, such as increased income payouts of two to three times the actual cash account value for long-term care needs. In fact, many annuity accounts also allow owners to withdraw funds from the account for these needs without incurring any surrender charge or penalty. For example, surrender charges might be waived if the annuity owner has been confined to a nursing home for a minimum time period or if the annuity owner is suffering a terminal type of illness.

Additional access to penalty-free funds could even be available for home health care, care-giving, or certain types of discounted long-term care services from a specific group of providers.

Increasing Income Payout Rider

An increasing income payout option, sometimes referred to as an inflation hedged option, will allow the annuity owner to purchase the annuity with a payout that will increase either based on a consumer price index growth every year or by a pre-determined fixed percentage, some also allow linked-index interest-earnings to be applied directly as an increased income stream each year.

With a level annuity payout, the annuitant will receive the same level amount for life. However, for those who are concerned about inflation, an inflation hedged annuity payout option could provide a good solution. With an increasing payout option, the annuity income payout may on some annuities start off at a lower amount and then it steadily increases over time.

The downside to choosing this option depending on the annuity and company is that it may take several years for the payout to reach a level that is equivalent to the initial payout on a level annuity payout. Laddering deferred annuities to start a higher level income at later intervals is also used effectively as an inflation hedge.

Increasing payouts are more of a hedge against inflation than a guarantee to keep up with or exceed inflation, since no one knows what the future of inflationary pressures will produce as a final result.

How Most Annuity Income Riders Work

Value	Cash Account Value	Income Account Value
How It Is Used	This is the cash account value for basic annuity calculations, including the value to be paid at death, surrender, for annuitized income or value at maturity. This is the true cash value of the annuity.	It has one primary purpose: it is the value or formula that is used to determine the lifetime guaranteed amount of each payment that may be minimally guaranteed by the annuity income rider. There is no cash account value here, this is only a rider accounting formula.
How It Grows	Any bonus is applied to the initial annuity purchase amount plus interest earnings periodically applied--using a choice of fixed rates or linked market index strategies for interest growth.	Any bonus is applied to the initial annuity purchase amount plus interest earnings periodically applied--then based on the sum of the above elements--income account growth is guaranteed at a contractual percentage while in deferral. Income is then determined based on the greater of the cash account value or the income account value. Income guarantee percentages paid out of the cash- or income-account value are determined by age.

Video: <u>Who Needs an Income Rider?</u>

<u>Click & Watch this video to find the answer...</u>

Video URL: http://annuityguys.com/annuity-income-riders

QR Codes for smart phones:

Chapter 10: Annuity Discussions

"Can you believe that we have been in meetings all week and we cannot even remember the annuities we discussed?! Oh well, we can always pick up where we left off this week -- next week!"

"Rule Number 1: Never lose money. Rule Number 2: Never forget rule No. 1." -Warren Buffett

Case Study 9 -- Jack and Mary

The day finally came when Jack and Mary, ages sixty-five and sixty-two, confirmed that they were in full agreement to retire since Mary was now eligible for Social Security. They had worked hard all of their lives, put the children through college, and helped the children out whenever they could.

After many discussions, Jack and Mary were ready to enjoy their retirement years. Hoping to have a comfortable and secure retirement, they wanted all of their recurring expenses to be covered by a safe stream of income. Jack and Mary were relying on two primary sources of reliable income. These included Jack's employer-sponsored pension and their Social Security retirement benefits. However, at that time, Jack and Mary fell $1,500 per month short of being able to pay all of their expenses--including, as they put it, their "fun money"--by using just these two income streams.

After careful consideration, Jack and Mary decided to fund an annuity that would provide them with a secure and guaranteed income to cover this shortfall in their recurring expenses. With an understanding how an annuity can be structured around their needs, they hoped to achieve two key parameters--the desire that Jack and Mary had for the $1,500 per month to be paid out for as long as either one of them are still living, and they wanted to make sure that any of the funds they did not use from an annuity's cash value would be paid penalty-free to their children when they passed on pre-maturely.

Using an annuity income calculator with the help their advisor, Jack and Mary calculated that it would take about $375,000 to create the $1,500 of joint income per month that they needed. Their annuity would have income guaranteed for life with a penalty free return of any unused cash account value to their children. This would allow them to achieve both of the parameters they had hoped to accomplish.

Jack and Mary elected to use a portion of Jack's 401(k) in order to make the allocations to their new MarketFree™ hybrid annuities. With this in place, this couple now have the additional income that they need to cover all of their fixed recurring retirement expenses for the rest of their lives plus some *"fun money!"*. This left about an equal amount of money to invest more aggressively for a hedge against inflation to create future income from when or if needed.

Video: <u>The Five Top Annuity Safety Risks</u>

<u>Click & Watch this video to learn about the risks...</u>

Video URL: http://annuityguys.com/the-five-top-annuity-safety-risks

QR Codes for smart phones:

Are Annuities Safe?

Safety of money is generally relative to comparing levels of risk between government-backed, insurance-backed, or market-oriented securities with no safety net.

In regard to non-variable MarketFree™ fixed annuities: State regulation forces insurance companies to follow what is known as statutory accounting, unlike generally accepted accounting principles (GAAP) utilized by publicly owned corporations. Statutory accounting is a *"show me the money"* type of accounting, whereby expenses are written off immediately and not capitalized to inflate profits for corporate convenience or even possible fraud. Most insurance carriers are also publicly traded companies that must also meet GAAP standards.

Insurance institutions are required to demonstrate to state regulatory authorities that dollar-for-dollar client's money (premium) is safely on deposit in secure financial vehicles such as investment-grade securities or government bonds. In addition, they are required to have reserves known as additional paid in surplus. The minimum amount of required reserves is decided based on the safety of the investments as determined by state regulators. So, based on these stringent requirements, insurance carriers are scrutinized and forced by law to meet and maintain a legal reserve for the safety of clients.

Each insurance carrier is also compelled to participate in a mandated state insurance guarantee association (SIGA), whereby insured clients typically have minimum guarantees on annuities and life insurance, ranging from $100,000 to $500,000 on annuities and life insurance; be aware that each state sets their own limits. These guarantees are not to be confused with FDIC insurance or used in sales or marketing of insurance products. A state's first concern is the safety of the client. So, if an insurer begins to have any serious financial concerns, the state places them in receivership and transfers ownership to a better managed and profitable carrier, with all assets moved over from the faltering insurance company. Thus, the faltering insurance company's clients remain whole and the guarantee association is absolved of any further monetary liability from the failed insurer.

Beyond this, third-party rating agencies examine these insurance institutions under a financial microscope. These rating agencies include A.M. Best, Moody's, Standard and Poor's, Fitch, Weiss, The Street, and several others. These ratings can be easily watched from year to year and typically vary slightly from one year to the next, so it is possible to detect a developing problem by way of a trend or pattern before an insurance carrier reaches any serious financial challenge that could affect that carrier's continued viability. These rating agencies produce detailed reports consisting of hundreds of pages of analysis from in-depth audits. They also summarize the insurer's near-term and long-term future rating outlook, typically as positive, negative, or stable.

An annuity's degree of safety is also dependent upon the specific type of annuity.

Variable Annuities for instance, are essentially considered to be investments in the securities market, which can be turbulent and unable to assure any type of security or safety to underlying principal, especially concerning a relied upon retirement nest egg.

While variable annuities offer tax deferral, as well as the ability to be annuitized for a lifetime income stream, these products are tied to variable equities. These equities are offered with the annuity in the form of mutual fund-type subaccounts. In fact, some variable annuities can have many different subaccounts in order to give the annuity owner a choice of investments to help meet specific investment goals and risk tolerance.

Variable annuity subaccounts can be comprised of stock offerings, bond funds, and even money market accounts. In addition, some variable annuities offer a fixed interest option as well.

MarketFree™ Fixed Annuities offers safety of principal and account value in retirement and a fixed rate of return for a fixed period of time. These financial instruments often resemble bank certificates of deposit in the way that they work. Here, the annuity purchaser places money into the annuity for a specified period of time, and the funds will grow with an agreed upon interest rate or a fluctuating declared (or current) interest rate which can vary from year to year. If the fixed annuity owner decides to pull money out prior to the end of the time period, the annuity owner may be assessed a penalty or surrender charge similar to the way CDs work.

Unlike bank CDs which are typically held for a much shorter period of time, a fixed annuity will have terms that may range from one to ten years or more. Also, CDs are FDIC protected, while annuities are not. Annuities, however, have many strong safety factors that need to be considered before choosing the one that is best.

The rate on a fixed annuity is typically guaranteed for one to ten years and can often be renewed at current rates on its anniversary date. Thus, fixed rate annuities can offer predictable safety to the retiree by protecting the principal while having at least a minimum guaranteed rate of return.

MarketFree™ Index Annuities, another annuity type with a minimum interest guarantee is a fixed index annuity (FIA) which allows one to protect his or her principal and earnings from market risk while benefiting from some of the market's upside. Therefore, one cannot lose principal and interest earnings even if the market index linked to the FIA declines since they have minimum guarantees. These annuities are designed to provide a higher potential interest return than other competitive types of safety-oriented savings vehicles like bank CDs and high quality bonds.

With an index annuity, since interest is linked to movements in a market index, there can be time periods when the index annuity is able to credit double-digit interest rates. Conversely, there can be other years where there is no interest earned at all. However, in design, index annuities were developed with the intent of offering a realistic potential for higher interest rates than other safe types of financial instruments that protect principal and earnings from market risk.

Thus the primary goal of the minimum interest guarantee is to protect an annuity owner's principal with some minimum growth. So, if the market does experience a consistent no-growth long-term decline, the worst thing that an index annuity owner can have happen is no gain or a minimal gain in principal. There are index annuities that credit a minimum amount of interest every year in the event the index never performs in the positive.

MarketFree™ Hybrid Annuities offer owners unique qualities of various different types of annuities. Hybrid annuities are, in most advisory circles understood to be, a fixed index annuity chassis with a newer generation income rider attached.

This fixed type of annuity is considered safe because it has upside market potential with no direct market exposure, and thus no downside market risk. In addition, hybrid annuities allow for heirs of the annuity owner to receive the full account value of what has not been spent by the owner-- even after the income rider is turned on for a lifetime of guaranteed payments. When the annuitant passes away before receiving an income, the entire account balance including all earnings and any bonus placed into the account, will be paid to heirs in-full and penalty-free.

Overall Annuity Safety Considerations

Overall, when people think about protecting money, the first thing that comes to mind for many is FDIC insurance. Federal Deposit Insurance Corporation (FDIC) is actually an insurance company that is backed by the United States government in order to help protect assets of up to $250,000 per person and per account in some circumstances.

Unlike bank deposits, annuities are not FDIC insured. However, annuities are offered by insurance companies whose primary purpose and expertise is to manage risk. When an individual owns a fixed annuity, funds are guaranteed and protected by the claims paying ability of the issuing insurance company.

An insurance company's number one objective and mandate is managing risk--it is the essence of what an insurance company does. In the case of annuities, the insurer's number one responsibility is to protect their clients' assets. Many insurance companies are a hundred or more years old, standing the test of time, prospering through recessions, depressions, wars, plagues, and many natural disasters.

Some factors prospective annuity owners may want to consider regarding insurance companies that offer annuities are the age and size of the insurance company in addition to the ratings earned from third party rating agencies. Insurance companies are rated and monitored based on their overall safety and financial solvency. A couple of key factors that these companies are rated on are the quality of their holdings and dollar amount of cash they keep in reserve to meet and exceed their obligations.

Two of the primary insurance company rating agencies are A.M. Best and Standard and Poor's. When seeking to allocate funds to an annuity, it is a good idea to look for issuing insurance companies that have at least an A.M. Best rating of A- in order to be certain beyond reasonable doubt that the company has a sufficient amount of assets in reserve to easily and fully protect, not just an annuity that may be considered, but all of their clients' annuities.

Video: <u>High Annuity Rates or Ratings?</u>

Click& Watch this video & find the balance...

Video URL: http://annuityguys.com/annuity-rates-or-ratings-what-is-more-important

QR Code for smart phones:

Annuity Satisfaction

With all of the advantages of annuities for retirees, there is a direct correlation between annuities and a sense of well-being in retirement. In fact, according to a survey in *Annuity Digest*, it appears that people who have access to the pension-style guaranteed lifetime income that comes from annuities may also be happier in retirement as well.

In a working paper written by Constantijn W.A. Panis, PhD, are details highlighting annuities and retirement well-being. It focuses on two measures--self-reported satisfaction with retirement and the number of self-reported depressive symptoms. The data in this paper came from a number of questions asked of survey respondents regarding well-being in retirement. One of these questions asked: "Has retirement turned out to be very satisfying, moderately satisfying, or not at all satisfying?" It also introduced a set of questions that were designed to assess symptoms of depression.

At a high level and not surprisingly, the study found that health and financial resources are the main factors driving retirement satisfaction. The study concludes that with respect to annuities and retirement satisfaction, there is a positive correlation. In other words, it was found that greater levels of annuity assets were related to greater levels of satisfaction throughout retirement. (hmmm, quality of life and financial security just might work well together!)

Annuities and Retirement

Tax treatment of annuities can be different, depending upon whether annuities are qualified or non-qualified. For example, non-qualified annuities--those that are funded with after-tax dollars--are not subject to IRS required minimum distribution (RMD) rules when the annuity owner reaches the age seventy and a half.

Qualified annuities are funded primarily by pretax dollars. Thus, funds in the annuity account will fall under the tax-qualified category. Here, typical qualified annuities include individual retirement annuities (IRAs) and some employer-sponsored retirement accounts, such as 401(k) or 403(b) plans.

Once qualified annuity owners reach age seventy and a half, the IRS requires that the owner take at least a minimum distribution each year from the annuity. This is referred to as a Required Mandatory Distribution or RMD. The amount of this RMD is calculated by the value of all of the qualified plan assets owned by the annuity holder, not just the tax-qualified annuity in question. It is required to use the IRS's actuarial table, found in Publication 590, which is based on life expectancy. Failure of the annuity holder to take the required distribution can result in a 50 percent tax penalty on the amount of money that was supposed to be distributed.

If a qualified annuity has not been annuitized, then the RMD must be based on the current account value of the annuity, in addition to the actuarial present value of any additional benefits that are provided under the annuity.

In the past, many annuity issuers used the annuity account value as the balance for the purpose of calculating RMD. However, regulations effective in 2006 provided that, if an annuity had not yet been annuitized, the annuity's value - for the purpose of the RMD - will be the annuity contract value plus the actuarial present value of any additional benefits that are provided under that annuity.

Non-qualified annuities, on the other hand, do not have RMDs required by tax law. The annuity income on non-qualified annuities is determined by the individual annuity owner, and payments are typically based on the annuitant's age as well as the value of the annuity, as pre-determined by actuarial tables.

Annuities and Tax

An annuity is a tax-deferred financial product. This means that the gains in the annuity will not be taxed each year on the earnings, it will however be taxed when any income is received from the annuity or a distribution it is taken as a withdrawal (which is considered income). The earnings are always taxed first, based on an IRS formula referred to as last-in, first-out (LIFO). Annuity owners can receive funds from annuities in a number of different ways including lump sum amounts, annuitized income, contractually guaranteed lifetime income based on an income rider, penalty free withdrawals, tax free long term care proceeds, and even death benefits (from deceased owners to beneficiaries).

The tax treatment of annuities has been subject to changes over the years. In some cases, not all of these changes have been favorable. However, a major advantage has remained in that the earnings growth within an annuity is non-taxable in the deferral phase of the annuity.

This can provide a great enhancement to the annuity's ability to grow at a much higher rate than other savings vehicles that are not tax deferred. With this, interest that is compounded with more interest, instead of leaving an account as a tax payment, accumulates net wealth at a considerably greater rate. All of the earnings that an annuity generates within the account value are fully available for ongoing growth creating more accumulation, since it is unhampered by tax payments.

If an annuity contract is fully surrendered during its accumulation phase, the owner will be responsible for paying income tax on any earnings in that contract. The owner is not, however, taxed on any amount that represents a return of the original principal used to purchase the annuity.

Partial withdrawals from an annuity during its accumulation phase are taxed on a last-in, first-out basis. This means that those withdrawals are made as earnings first, and the owner will be taxed until all of the earnings have been withdrawn.

Note that there is one exception to the earnings-first rule for contributions made to an annuity contract prior to August 14, 1982. These contributions will be distributed on a first-in, first-out basis, so, the owner will not be taxed until the initial principal allocations are fully recovered.

MarketFree™ Fixed Annuities and Tax

Fixed annuities are considered to be tax-deferred annuities. These contracts are officially between an individual and an insurance company that provides a guaranteed principal and interest-bearing annuity policy, which also includes standard annuitization for lifetime income and some optional riders may be available for additional guaranteed income or other retirement benefits.

The insurance company will pay interest on a fixed annuity, but the annuity owner is not responsible for paying tax on interest earned until the owner/annuitant begins making random withdrawals or begins receiving a systematic income from the annuity.

Fixed annuities usually earn fairly competitive above average rates of return. Since these annuities are tax-deferred, owners can earn even more with compounding interest on the earnings than would otherwise have been paid in tax to, *YOU guessed it*, Uncle Sam!

Over time, tax-deferred growth has the ability to considerably outpace taxable investments. This is due to the fact that the earnings compound without taxation, year in and year out. This is not so with most other investments such as CDs, some bond interest or short-term stock dividends, which are taxable each year regardless of whether the growth from these are withdrawn or left in the account. Non-annuity taxable accounts send 1099s in January of each year so tax due can be figured and paid on taxable accounts; unlike annuities that have no tax due or 1099 reporting required.

Variable Annuities and Taxes

A variable annuity can offer many advantages. One of the biggest benefits to variable annuities is their favorable tax treatment. In fact, compared to that of other investments such as mutual funds, one of the big reasons why many investors choose a variable annuity is for the growth of long-term retirement investments that can be traded inside the annuity with no taxable event.

In addition, variable annuities are appealing to those in higher tax brackets who seek tax-favored ways of accumulating wealth, especially if one anticipates that the tax rate will drop once retirement is reached and it is time to slowly access the annuity funds. Variable annuities remain one of the few investment vehicles outside of a tax-qualified retirement plan to be given tax-deferred accumulation treatment especially in regard to holding securities.

The funds that are invested into a variable annuity are considered the contract's initial principal and basis for tax purposes. Unless these funds were deducted or exempted from income tax as a tax qualified annuity, example; IRA-401K-403B-etc., when they were contributed or rolled-over into an annuity, the basis will not be subject to tax when withdrawals are made.

With a variable annuity, the interest or growth on the annuity's principal, however, will be subject to tax when it is withdrawn or distributed as systematic income.

Taxation of Lump Sum Distributions

If the owner of an annuity decides to take a lump sum distribution from an annuity account, then one will receive the entire value of the contract less any surrender charge, if applicable. This option is likely the least effective from a tax-planning standpoint since the annuity owner will have a liability for paying tax on all of the annuity earnings in a single year, which effectively can place one into a higher tax bracket, thus increasing the tax bill substantially. In addition, the annuity owner will also have lost the benefit of ongoing tax-deferred growth.

Taxation of Annuity Living Benefits

Annuity living benefits have become very popular over the last few years, as more and more individuals have become wary about placing assets at risk in the market. Many of the living benefit options have been designed to help in providing protection from poor market performance and low interest rates.

For example, the guaranteed minimum withdrawal benefit (GMWB) on a variable annuity is an option that allows annuity owner to protect future income against downside market risk. This option may also allow the annuitant the right to withdraw a maximum percentage of guaranteed income every year and hopefully recoup the amount of the initial investment and then some. All gains must come out first, which are taxable at ordinary federal income tax rates.

Withdrawals will be considered as being taxable until the gains have been drawn down to the cost basis that remains in the contract, based on LIFO. After the cost basis is depleted and income is still available, then any withdrawals will be considered as taxable earnings again and will also be subject to possible withholding.

Another living benefit -the guaranteed minimum income benefit (GMIB) guarantees annuity owners--once the annuity has been annuitized-- to receive a minimum lifetime income of annuitized payments from the contract. This type of payout has an exclusion ratio calculated by the insurer based on an IRS formula which determines the portion of the income that is non-taxable.

Taxation of Annuity Death Benefits

If an annuity owner passes away prior to the annuitization of an annuity contract, the annuity contract will provide for a death benefit to be paid to a beneficiary(s). Unlike life insurance, the death benefit paid under the annuity contract may not be received tax-free by the beneficiary(s). In addition, the annuity will not grant a step-up in basis to the beneficiary(s). The amount that is considered taxable to the beneficiary is the amount of the death benefit that exceeds the contract's original contribution amount. A Roth Individual Retirement Annuity is an exception and the death- or income- benefit is 100 percent tax free.

The death benefit from an annuity may be taken as a lump sum or over a period of time. It may, in most cases, also be annuitized over the lifetime of the beneficiary(s), or it can be distributed fully over five years from the original annuity owner's death. The beneficiary(s) will owe income tax on a portion of the earnings determined by an exclusion ratio as the income payments from the annuity are paid, if annuitized.

Extending the receipt of the income payments over time will enable the beneficiary(s) to spread out the tax liability. If the beneficiary(s) is the annuity owner's spouse, then the tax rules will allow the spouse to take ownership of the annuity contract avoiding taxation as a withdrawal and continue the accumulation if so desired by the spouse.

If the annuity owner passes away after the annuity's annuitization phase has begun, then the remaining payments, if there are any left that are contractually guaranteed, they will be paid out to the beneficiary(s) under the annuity payout option that was in effect at the time of the annuity owner's death. In this case, the taxable and nontaxable portions of such payments will continue to be determined by the annuity's original exclusion ratio.

Other Annuity Withdrawal Considerations

Since the passage of the Tax Equity and Fiscal Responsibility Act (TEFRA) in 1982, withdrawals from annuities are treated on a last-in, first-out (LIFO) basis. This simply means that whatever is considered as going into the annuity contract last--in this case, the annuity's interest earnings--is deemed to be first to be withdrawn for tax purposes. Therefore, annuity withdrawals are completely taxable to the extent that the contract has accumulated growth.

TEFRA also imposed another provision on annuity withdrawals. That is, the earnings in most scenarios may not be withdrawn without penalty until the annuity owner reaches age fifty-nine and a half, except in very specific circumstances--a penalty exception is made for life immediate annuities. This 10 percent penalty is applied to the earnings of the annuity withdrawal or the portion that is taxable. Therefore, the penalty is not imposed on any of the principal amount that is being withdrawn.

Under some very limited criteria, the 10 percent penalty for early annuity withdrawals will be waived such as:

- Death
- 72T substantially equal payments
- Annuitization
- Spousal Continuation for Income
- Life Immediate Annuities

With the 72T exception, the annuity owner can also avoid the 10 percent penalty if one takes some or all of the annuity distributions in a series of substantially equal payments based on a formula that limits the amount of income allowed under the 72T IRS-IRC provision.

In addition, the Pension Protection Act of 2006 provided that, beginning in 2010, withdrawals from nonqualified annuities that are used to pay for a long-term care needs, based on certain annuities with specific long-term care protections, may not be subject to taxation.

Annuities & Estate Tax

For purposes of federal estate tax, the general rule is that an annuity's value will be included in the owner's gross estate. If the annuity owner is to pass away prior to the annuitization period of the annuity, then the full value of that annuity will be included in the estate.

If, however, the annuity owner is to pass away after the annuitization has begun and remaining values of the annuity are paid to a beneficiary(s), then the amount that will be included in the annuity owner's estate will be the present value of the future annuity payments.

Video: <u>Annuities & Estate Planning</u>

<u>Click & Watch this video before using annuities in estate planning...</u>

Video URL: http://annuityguys.com/annuities-can-they-be-used-effectively-in-estate-planning

QR Code for smart phones:

Rollovers & Annuities

An annuity to annuity rollover, referred to as a 1035 exchange specifically used for non-tax-qualified annuities, allows for the direct transfer of an annuity from one insurance company to another without incurring an IRS imposed tax penalty or taxable event. As long as the funds go directly from one company to another, there will be no taxes due on that exchange. However, if the owner/annuitant actually takes receipt of the funds, then he or she could incur considerable tax consequences.

This type of exchange has different rules than IRA rollovers which can also be done by rolling over an annuity to another annuity, or from other types of accounts into annuities. However, with IRA rollovers, it is okay to take possession of the money as long as it is repositioned back into a tax-qualified retirement account within sixty days known as sixty-day rollovers. Inherited IRAs are an exception to the sixty day rollover. Funds must be moved from custodian to custodian to avoid a taxable event.

The ability to make 1035 exchanges is an important tax benefit that annuities can offer. At any point that it is advantageous, an annuity owner has the option to upgrade to a different annuity contract that is more appropriate to the annuity owners needs at that time.

In keeping with the assurance that the 1035 exchange remains a non-taxable event, there are a few rules that an annuity owner must follow. These are:

- The new and the old annuity contracts must be non-qualified.
- The new and the old annuity contracts must have the same owner; with some insurance companies, they must also have the same annuitant. (After the actual exchange has taken place, however, the owner and the annuitant can be changed).
- The exchange must take place between the insurance company that issued the old annuity contract and the insurance company that is issuing the new annuity contract. The owner of the annuity is not allowed to take possession of any of the funds that are being transferred. Thus, the exchange is carried out by assigning the original contract to the new insurance company in exchange for the issuance of a new annuity contract.

- If the annuity owner is to receive any of these funds directly, then the transaction will be considered an annuity surrender. Any gain in that annuity account will be considered to be taxable. Also, if the annuity owner is younger than age fifty-nine and a half, a 10 percent tax penalty on any earnings may also apply.

An annuity rollover is not required to involve two different insurance companies. In fact, an annuity that is issued by one insurance company can be exchanged for another annuity that is issued by the same company. With the new annuity, the values will remain the same as they were in the old annuity. This also means that the same proportion of invested principal and interest earnings that the previous contract contained will carry over to the new annuity.

Annuity owners can also make partial exchanges with their annuities. The IRS has deemed these exchanges as also being tax-free, provided that certain guidelines are followed with regard to how the cost basis and the gain of the amounts in the new annuity will be treated. Essentially, the IRS states that all values retain the same proportion of principal to earnings as they held in the original annuity prior to the exchange.

It should be noted, however, that the IRS very closely views partial 1035 exchanges to determine whether or not they are being used as a way to avoid taxes on annuity withdrawals. This is because the IRS is concerned due to the fact that a partial annuity exchange can alter or confuse the amount of funds in an annuity that are subject to tax upon withdrawal. The IRS is wary that annuity owners may be able to abuse the tax laws in the partial exchanges.

Video: <u>Avoid Tax On IRA & 401K Rollovers!</u>

<u>Click & Watch this video to learn how...</u>

Video URL: http://annuityguys.com/avoid-tax-on-iras-and-401ks-moving-to-annuities

QR Code for smart phones:

FIAs & Hybrids: Buy-or-Beware

In some ways, MarketFree™ hybrids--basically a fixed index annuity (FIA) can offer their owners the best of both worlds, especially when coupled with a progressive income rider, a guarantee of principal with the potential of market-linked growth, and no risk to principal or earnings loss when market downturns occur. In other words, they offer protection of principal, higher potential growth, some have a long-term care benefit, majority control of the annuity account value, protection from probate for heirs, and a guaranteed pension style income regardless of economic conditions.

Due to MarketFree™ fixed index annuities' stock market indexing strategies, they can even bring a conservative annuity owner extra interest while avoiding all market risk. And in the case of flat or down markets, fixed index annuities can bring considerably better growth than the indexes they are correlated too. In fact, between 1999 and 2010 according to the 2009-2010 Wharton study, many fixed index annuities actually outperformed the indices which they were correlated to. This index correlation or linking is part of the formula used to determine how much interest will be earned based on a specified period of time.

Principal safety and an opportunity to benefit from market gains make fixed index annuities quite attractive in today's uncertain economy. During the accumulation phase of a fixed index annuity, one has the opportunity to benefit from some portion of stock market gains while principal is protected against stock market losses.

The FIA contract will typically guarantee a minimum rate of interest on the account value while the annuity is growing. The issuing insurance company will credit the annuity with either the minimum interest that is stated in the annuity contract or interest that is based on the performance of the linked index.

FIAs give individuals all of the features of a fixed annuity including tax-deferred growth, an income stream, and even a death benefit. Some benefits of fixed index annuities include:

- Safety - These annuities are backed by highly regulated insurance companies;

- Tax-deferred growth;
- Higher returns - FIAs typically provide better interest rates than CDs and standard fixed annuities;
- Death benefit payout guarantee even in the lifetime income phase;
- Liquidity - FIAs generally offer flexible withdrawal privileges;
- Unlimited contributions - Unlike an IRA or a 401(k), FIA will allow unlimited contributions to the account;
- Inheritance - FIAs allow money to pass directly to heirs, bypassing probate;
- Lifetime income option - FIAs provide income that cannot be outlived by way of annuitization or income riders.

Given all of the benefits of FIAs, there are a few disadvantages that must be considered which include:

- A possible 10 percent tax penalty on withdrawals of earnings by the annuity owner who is below age fifty-nine and a half;
- Early withdrawal penalties or surrender charges for large withdrawals prior to maturity or when withdrawing in excess of the 10 percent annual surrender-free portion;
- Ordinary income tax owed on earnings during the withdrawal or income payout stage;
- Last in, first out (LIFO) tax requirement. Earnings are taxed first, unless annuitization takes place, and then a tax exclusion ratio is used;
- FIAs are not FDIC insured;
- FIAs do not capture the full upside of the stock market;
- Caps, participation, spreads, and declared fixed interest rates may be subject to change on an annual basis;
- It is possible during a down year(s) to have zero-interest crediting.

Individuals, therefore, who may need money prior to retirement may prefer a CD, a money market account, or a securities-oriented investment in order to avoid a surrender penalty from the annuity issuer or the potential 10 percent tax penalty on earnings that is imposed for taking money out of an annuity prior to the age fifty-nine and a half. For individuals who are at or near retirement, fixed annuities may be a better choice.

There are many considerations that may be relative to someone's own unique and specific situation. A fixed index annuity that works for a fifty-year-old single mother may be a bad decision for a younger married couple.

It is important to understand that no one hybrid or fixed index annuity will give retirees everything that is needed or desired. Hence, it is necessary to prioritize one's needs. For those considering a fixed index-/hybrid-annuity, there are some key factors to think about, including:

- High independent ratings for safety;
- High interest crediting for growth;
- Generous payouts for income;
- Adequate liquidity for emergency cash needs;
- Reasonable surrender periods and fair surrender charges;
- Additional benefits (riders) such as payouts for long-term care, terminal illness, and death benefits;
- Flexible income riders that allow both lifetime income and the ability to pass any remaining account value to heirs;
- More indexing options for higher growth potential;
- Better indexing strategies for higher growth potential;
- Higher cap rates, higher participation, higher averaging
- A larger bonus;
- No- or low- annual-fees;
- Shorter versus longer resets to grow and protect accumulation;
- High water mark interest crediting versus annual point-to-point;
- Higher deferred growth of the income base and higher percentages on age based payouts;
- Availability of the income base for a death benefit;
- Joint survivor income guarantees with the option to elect when and if needed to optimize life income if a spouse is unexpectedly pre-deceased.

All fixed index annuities are tax deferred with no income tax requirements until withdrawal. This is a definite advantage over many investments, like CDs, mutual funds, stocks, and bonds, when considering a long-term financial vehicle.

A long-term fixed index annuity allocation has the potential to outperform CDs, bonds, and treasuries. Reinvesting money that would otherwise be paid out in tax over an extended period of years is always an advantage. In addition, fixed index annuities have several benefits that can also be important for retirement planning.

Video: Top Ten Hybrid Annuity Questions

Click & Watch this video to find out the top ten hybrid annuity questions you must get answers to...

Video URL: http://annuityguys.com/ten-questions-to-ask-before-purchasing-a-hybrid-annuity

QR Code for smart phones:

Understanding MarketFree Pre-Issued Annuities™

For many retirees in this low interest rate environment, given the choice between the new and Pre-Issued, the answer is a resounding YES to the latter!

Interestingly, Pre-Issued Annuities ™ are in fact not even an annuity! The purchaser actually buys a stream of payments sold by the owner of the original annuity through a court order process that protects the purchaser as the new and rightful owner of the payment stream purchased. Pre-Issued Annuities ™ are fully backed by the same financial strength of the Insurance company or companies that issued the original annuity to the owner and/or annuitant.

Positive Attributes - Pre-Issued Annuities™

- High Yields - typically 4.5 to 7.5 percent;
- Safety - payment streams are guaranteed by highly rated insurance companies; Court order process protects both buyer and seller; Issuers are regulated by State Insurance Commissions with guarantee associations;
- Fixed and reliable income streams;
- Diversification for portfolios of more sophisticated investors;
- Truly a non-market correlated asset;
- IRA or Qualified Account compatibility;
- Estate transfer to heirs;
- Twenty year plus successful transaction history;

Negative Attributes - Pre-Issued Annuities™

- Limited liquidity selling payment streams prior to maturity could result in a considerable loss;
- The court order process should be monitored by an expert attorney;
- The best Pre-Issued Annuities ™ usually never make it to the internet or retail lists;

- The industry is controlled by a few power players catering mostly to institutional investors;
- Contracts may require a 10% to 20% escrow to secure future ownership during the court order process, tying up money at low or no interest for up to 90 days;
- Approximately thirty percent of initiated contracts get rejected by the court and escrow is returned;
- The industry has commission oriented sales people that will sometimes promise too much and then fall short on delivery. Some may prefer for the client to not use an expert attorney;
- Contracts are often discounted too far away from the source of funds diluting potential yield;
- Many contracts available on the internet are older inventory that has been passed over by others;
- Life contingent contracts can end abruptly with an insurance company paying back principal and yield early since the annuitant died unexpectedly;
- Not FDIC insured.

Pre-Issued Annuity™ Safety & Yield

Once the high yielding yet safe nature of these financial vehicles is understood, it becomes apparent that most retirees have money that would be well suited to this type of strategy. The biggest question most individual investors have is "how do I get started without making any regrettable mistakes?"

The key is using an expert who specializes in this field, having a sincere interest towards the client. The best advisor for this will have experience in the industry and inside sources for access to the best available contracts. At times, it is also important to use an attorney with expertise in this arena to follow and assure the validity of the court order process.

Pre-Issued Annuity™ Experts

Unfortunately, most advisors and attorneys who have the all around qualifications needed have already been hired or retained at the firms that harvest these payment streams. It is important to find an independent attorney who is an expert to look after the client's interests.

Factoring companies that sell Pre-Issued Annuities ™ mostly always pay someone a commission. The attorney is the safety net; a skilled professional who has a vested interest in a client's success. And just like any licensed advisor, an attorney could lose his or her license to practice if he or she does not act in the client's best interest

Ask those in the industry for a list of independent attorneys with expertise in the discipline of Pre-Issued Annuities ™.

Pre-Issued Annuity™ Advantages

- Typically a high Annual Percentage Yield of 4.5% to 7.5%;
- Predictable future income or lump sum payments;
- Payment stream is transferable to heirs;
- Allows income based on yield with the ability to recapture the original principal.

Pre-Issued Annuity™ Disadvantages

- Lack of liquidity beyond the scheduled payment stream or future lump sum payouts;
- When liquidated prior to maturity losses can be substantial;
- Lack of flexibility to structure as needed. It must be accepted as offered;
- Involves a court order process which commonly takes up to ninety days;
- Escrow may be required of approximately 10% to 20% when committing to a particular Pre-Issued Annuity ™;

- It is possible to have the court order process fail and have to start anew after the escrow is refunded;
- Higher yielding life contingent contracts may be paid in full prior to the specified principal, and yield due to date if the annuitant dies prematurely. The balance of funds returned will need to be reallocated to reach the originally desired objectives;
- An expert attorney should be retained to assure a successful and accurate transfer of ownership;
- Too many un-experienced salespeople lacking the expertise or resources needed to deliver the best available choice.

Pre-Issued Annuity ™ vs. Hybrid Annuity

Both of these annuities are unique in what they accomplish and occasionally in some ways, may overlap each other with similar results. The Pre-Issued Annuity ™ is better suited to a higher yield than standard fixed annuities or fixed index annuities - frequently referred to as hybrid annuities. The hybrid annuity on the other hand is better suited than the Pre-Issued Annuity ™ at providing a pension styled income that can never be outlived. Hybrid Annuities protect better against longevity risk, and when left in deferral it typically will produce a higher future income with guarantees for the security of never running out of future income.

Pre-Issued Annuity ™ and Hybrid Annuity Shared Advantages

- Safety - each are typically backed by highly rated insurance companies and tightly regulated by state insurance commissions with guarantee associations;
- IRA compatible;
- Can be inherited;
- Non securities correlated assets;
- Remove market volatility;
- Tax advantaged growth on any remaining balance;

- Give Peace of Mind in Retirement.

Pre-Issued Annuity™ and Hybrid Annuity and Shared Disadvantages

- Limited Liquidity;
- No FDIC protection;
- Best results only happen when held to maturity with Pre-Issued Annuities ™ or beyond with Hybrids.

Video: Pre Issued Annuities™ Safety & Yield

Click & Watch this two part video series to learn more...

Video URL's: http://annuityguys.com/annuity-types/pre-issued-annuities

QR Code for smart phones:

Chapter 11: Advisor Ethics and Standards

"Don't lecture me! I teach ethics classes all day long to stockbrokers. Haven't you heard of, "Do as I say, not as I do?"

"Even the most rational approach to ethics is defenseless if there isn't the will to do what is right." -Alexander Solzhenitsyn

Case Study 10 -- Tim and Martha

Tim and Martha were approaching retirement and were looking to invest some of their assets, approximately $500,000 into a financial strategy that would provide them safety while also having the potential for higher growth in order to keep up with inflation over time.

After hearing a real estate investor speak to a large group at a local hotel, the couple decided that they would set an appointment with the advisor to learn more about how they might participate. The advisor told Tim and Martha about his secure high earning real estate investment fund that promised them both maximum capital growth, with an emphasis on preservation of principal.

Fortunately, just prior to investing, they both found out that the advisor, who had yet to receive their $500,000, had been using investors' money to run a Ponzi scheme in which early investors were paid with later investors' funds.

The money the advisor had collected from his victims had also been used to support his lavish lifestyle that included many luxuries and gambling trips. The advisor was soon arrested and eventually was convicted.

Ethics for Advisors

Being a financial advisor is an honorable profession that is dishonored when its practitioners employ abusive sales practices. The root causes of abusive or unethical practices are lack of character and integrity which can manifest in its worst case scenario as a criminal action on the part of an advisor defrauding a client. This type of self-serving behavior can obviously be devastating to any investor, many times doing irreparable damage.

In order to be successful in the ethical realm of retirement planning using insurance and investment options, advisors must conduct their planning sessions and or investment advice in a manner that incorporates the client as a willing and able participant. In addition, financial advisors should always conduct their financial planning as a process to help protect and potentially grow clients' assets or to produce secure retirement income when needed.

This means understanding the true differences between clients' wants and needs, as well as any aversion to risk.

With this in mind, advisors must understand that many financial options available may not be the most suitable or appropriate solution for a certain client's financial need. If a financial option is not in a client's best interest, then the advisor should not encourage it. However, educating clients about any financial instrument they are curious about or interested in is the financial advisor's responsibility unless he or she lacks knowledge concerning a particular area of the client's concern or interest. Advisors should not be expected to be experts in every area of financial knowledge and the advisor should disclose if he is not knowledgeable or if expertise is lacking in particular areas of client concern or curiosity.

When advisors do offer various investments and services, they should be careful to not indulge in speaking poorly about other advisors' products, services, or business character unless it involves proven criminal or civil activity that is public knowledge and brought up by a client. Rather, an ethical advisor obviously must focus on his or her own merits and ability to benefit clients or prospective clients. Nor should the advisor ever use misleading or deceitful language in advertising when marketing investments and services.

The Securities and Exchange Commission (SEC) has developed a code of ethics for advisors and advisory firms to follow. This is detailed in SEC Rule 204A-1, issued under the Investment Advisers Act of 1940, requiring all registered investment advisors to adopt a code of ethics. This rule requires that all SEC-registered investment advisors create a written code of ethics to set forth the standards of business conduct that is to be expected of the investment advisor's "supervised persons," and it must address personal securities trading by those individuals as well.

According to this rule, an investment advisor's code of ethics must include the following:

- A standard or standards of business conduct that the investment advisor requires of its supervised persons that reflect the advisor's fiduciary obligations;

- Provisions that require the advisor's supervised persons to comply with applicable federal securities laws;
- Provisions that require all of the investment advisor's access persons to report their personal securities transactions and holdings at certain regular intervals, as well as reviewing of these transactions by the investment advisor firm;
- Provisions stating that all supervised persons must report any violations of the investment advisor's code of ethics promptly to the chief compliance officer;
- A requirement for the advisor to provide each of its supervised persons with a copy of the investment advisor's code of ethics and any amendments, and also a requirement that these supervised persons provide the investment advisor with a written acknowledgement of their receipt of the code of ethics as well as any amendments.

Also, the state- and SEC-registered investment advisors are required to establish, maintain, and enforce written policies and procedures that are reasonably designed to prevent the misuse of material non-public or insider information.

In addition to the general ethical principles that an advisor must follow, there is also a need to pay close attention to unfair marketing practices with relation to conduct in promoting financial and insurance-related products and services. These include:

- **Misrepresentation.** A financial advisor may not use misleading or incorrect information in the sale of financial or insurance-related products.
- **False advertising.** A financial advisor may not use any marketing materials with the intention of stating falsehoods or half-truths.
- **Defamation.** It is unethical to damage the character or the reputation of competitors or their products.
- **Twisting or Churning.** A financial services representative may suggest that a client let an existing insurance policy or annuity lapse so that the advisor may sell the client another similar product. This is WRONG--**unless** it makes good financial sense for the client to do so.

- **Rebating.** Offering a customer an inducement to purchase insurance is considered to be unethical and is even illegal in some states. For example, an insurance sales agent is employing rebating when the agent offers to pay for a client's vacation or to return a portion of the policy premium from an earned commission.
- **Bait and switch.** This practice consists of using a bargain-priced item to attract clients, and then encouraging the client to purchase a higher priced one. It has been used, illegally, to lure potential insurance clients who might not otherwise be inclined to respond.

Required Code of Ethics for Advisors

Financial service firms typically have required standards for advisors. Most firms have their own code of ethics that advisors must abide by, or face termination of further affiliation or employment with that firm.

An example of one firm's code of ethics for advisors:

- Advisors are never to make contact unwelcomed or uninvited.
- The advisor's responsibility is to offer answers to satisfy an individual's financial concerns.
- Advisors are required to supply and verify, upon request, the documents validating compliance with the firm's requirements as a selected advisor.
- Advisors will at all times be fully truthful with all individuals seeking financial guidance and assistance.
- The advisor must work in a spirit of full cooperation, always looking out for the highest and best interest of all individuals seeking assistance.
- The advisor will always make full disclosure of known available options and never knowingly withhold information that potentially could add a benefit or cause any harm.
- Any and all conflicts of interest will be immediately and fully disclosed.

- Advertising, marketing, and presentation materials will be truthful, suitable for the client's full understanding, and compliant with state and federal standards and regulations.
- Market performance, potential returns, and levels of risk must be stated realistically and truthfully.
- In the event that specific legal, financial, or tax advice is needed that exceeds the advisor's expertise, the advisor will willingly defer to a properly qualified professional.
- Continuing education as required by law and credentials will be ongoing. Advisors must stay current with changes in the financial landscape.

Video: <u>Finding a Great Retirement Advisor</u>

<u>Click & Watch this video for tips on choosing a great retirement advisor...</u>

Video URL: <u>http://annuityguys.com/how-to-choose-a-great-retirement-advisor</u>

QR Code for smart phones:

Chapter 12: SEC & FINRA - Friend or Foe?

"This our best trap for those Madoff-style rats. We perfected it on little stockbroker mice. Our goal is tricking the trickster!"

"Honesty is the best policy... when there's money in it."
-Mark Twain

Case Study 11 -- Robert and Sarah

Nowhere have we seen the devastating effects of noncompliance in the financial services world as we have in the recent case of Bernie Madoff. Thousands of investors have been affected, to the tune of an estimated $50 billion in fraudulent transactions. Many of those investors have lost their entire life savings in the supposedly golden retirement years.

For instance, the case of Robert and Sarah--pre-retirees who received a phone call back in December of 2008 letting them know that they were financially wiped out after forty years of diligent saving and investing

Sarah's entire family had been invested in a Madoff fund for decades and had lived very well on the consistent returns of between 15 and 22 percent annually. Now, all clients were victims and wiped out including retirees, those living off trusts, students with college funds, and a whole host of others.

Most would not have even guessed that the entire Madoff plan was just one big Ponzi scheme. Certainly, there were the usual warnings prior to investing regarding risk and return potential, as well as the typical concerns about staying well diversified and if "it sounds too good to be true"(dubious), it probably is.

However, the Madoff fund had been going so strong for so many years. Most investors didn't think twice about placing large chunks of retirement funds in it. In fact, even the Securities and Exchange Commission had apparently felt the fund was legitimate, allowing Madoff to continue operating after alleged fraud complaints and several audits.

A wide variety of small to large investors; along with hedge funds, global banks, institutions, and even pension funds, eventually became victims to this smooth con-man and his greed.

Insurance and Investment Regulation

In "watching over" the companies that offer annuities to the public, there are various organizations that assist the public in not only policing the products themselves but also the advisors who offer them. Annuities are regulated as an insurance product; however, variable annuities possess features of both life insurance and securities. Therefore, these annuities are subject to regulation by the Securities and Exchange Commission (SEC) as securities under federal securities laws. For example:

- Fixed annuities and Fixed Index Annuities (Hybrids) are not considered securities and therefore are not regulated as a security.
- Variable annuities have a securities aspect and therefore are regulated by the SEC. In this case, the SEC requires that all details, charges and fees applicable to a variable annuity be described in great detail in a prospectus, which must be offered to every investor who purchases a variable annuity.

Only insurance companies or fraternal organizations are allowed to issue annuity contracts issued to consumers and both are regulated by each individual state. This is why certain annuities or annuity options are not available in each state.

The IRS has a say in the taxation of annuity products. For instance, annuity contracts are defined by the Internal Revenue Code, which in turn governs their federal tax treatment.

Insurance companies and their agents are regulated by state insurance regulators.

The two bodies that are most commonly referred to with regard to investment regulation are the Securities and Exchange Commission (SEC) and the Financial Industry Regulatory Authority (FINRA). FINRA is a federally authorized self regulating organization (SRO).

Securities and Exchange Commission (SEC)

The Securities and Exchange Commission (SEC) is the primary federal regulatory agency for the securities industry. Its responsibility is to promote full disclosure of securities to the public as well as to protect investors against fraudulent and manipulative practices in the securities markets.

The SEC is responsible for enforcing, among other legislation, the Securities Act of 1933, the Securities Exchange Act of 1934, the Trust

Indenture Act of 1939, the Investment Company Act of 1940, and the Investment Advisers Act.

The SEC is made up of five commissioners. Each of these commissioners is appointed for a five-year term that is staggered so that one new commissioner is replaced every year. No more than three members of the commission can be of a single political party.

In addition, the SEC is comprised of four primary divisions which include:

- The Division of Corporate Finance which is responsible for making sure that all publicly traded companies disclose the required financial information to investors.
- The Division of Market Regulation oversees all legislation that involves brokers and brokerage firms.
- The Division of Investment Management is responsible for regulating the mutual fund and investment advisor industries.
- The Division of Enforcement enforces the securities legislation and investigates possible violations.

When choosing a financial advisor to help with one's investment decisions concerning securities, it is important to be sure that the financial offerings are regulated and that the advisors are in good standing and reputable. After all, when dealing with one's life savings, investors want to be sure that their funds are in the best hands possible.

While most financial professionals are honest, there are a few unscrupulous individuals in every industry, and financial services are no exception. Therefore, one must watch out for bad advisors in order to protect his or her assets. Often, even if a dishonest financial professional is stopped, the money from investors that is lost will potentially be gone forever. That is why it is so important to try to prevent this type of thing from happening in the first place.

One way to do this is by making sure that the investment professional one is considering working with is properly registered with the SEC or licensed to do business in a particular state. And investors can take it a step further and find out from the securities regulator in any state if the investment advisor or the advisory firm has ever had disciplinary actions, or any types of client or consumer complaints that are on file.

Furthermore, individuals should also try to find out as much as possible about any investment that an advisor is recommending. Find out if the recommended investments are registered. Although not all financial instruments are required to be registered, it is still wise to find out as much as is possible about the proposal.

One should certainly always be somewhat wary about any promise of quick profits, as well as any pressure from a financial services representative about purchasing a particular investment. On top of this, it is important to ask one's representative for any written materials including a prospectus, prior to investing any money. In fact, prior to making any investment, be sure that it is known and understood:

- How the investment will make money;
- How the investment is consistent with specific financial goals;
- What needs to happen for the investment to go up in value;
- What the risks are related to any particular investment;
- Where can additional information be found or verified.

When individuals decide to work with a particular investment professional, one should write down what the investment professional states regarding specific investments and other pertinent details. Good notes could come in handy if there ever is a problem in the future.

Financial Industry Regulatory Authority (FINRA)

The Financial Industry Regulatory Authority, or FINRA, is a regulatory body that was created after the merger of the National Association of Securities Dealers (NASD) and the New York Stock Exchange's (NYSE) regulation committee. FINRA is responsible for governing business between brokers, dealers, and the investing public. By consolidating these two regulators, FINRA's aim is to eliminate regulatory overlap and cost inefficiencies.

FINRA is an independent, not-for-profit organization that is empowered by the federal government to protect investors from fraud and bad practices in the financial services industry. Since variable annuities are considered securities, they are regulated by FINRA.

FINRA BrokerCheck

FINRA offers a way for consumers and investors to check out the background of advisors and firms. BrokerCheck is an informational vehicle that offers statistics on both past and present securities brokers and firms that are or were registered with FINRA. Use the website www.finra.org/brokercheck to find disciplinary actions taken against brokers and registered representatives. Use www.adviserinfo.sec.gov for registered investment advisor firms and investment advisor representatives with disciplinary actions.

By using BrokerCheck, individuals can learn about the history of a financial firm, learn positive facts and also about any indiscretions by a firm or advisor.

BrokerCheck was actually created by the Central Registration Depository (CRD), and the database holds information on over 660,000 brokers and firms, as well as numerous brokers and firms that were previously registered. The website is also very user-friendly in that it offers tools on how to best use the site and the information that is provided on it.

Check Out Brokers & Investment Advisors

Before placing money with any broker or financial advisor, it is a good idea to do some research. Doing so could literally change the course of someone's future retirement lifestyle, if it means avoiding an advisor with a not-so-positive track record or choosing one who can substantially enhance one's financial well-being.

Both state and federal securities laws require that brokers, investment advisors, and their firms be licensed or registered. In addition, important information must be made available to the public by advisors and his or her firm.

Mid-size investment advisors who have assets under management of at least $25 to $100 million are typically required to register with the SEC. If the amount of assets under management is below this figure, then advisors must register with the state securities agency in the state where the primary place of business is located.

With investment advisors who employ other financial representatives, they must make sure that those reps are licensed or registered with the state securities regulator in order to conduct business with clients.

Individual investors should do their due diligence prior to investing. One such way of conducting research is using the online services of the Central Registration Depository (CRD). The CRD website is a digital database that has information about most securities brokers, investment advisors, their representatives, and the firms that the advisor works for. For example, if someone wanted to find out if a securities broker or investment advisor is properly licensed to do business in a particular state, then this information, along with any complaints the advisor has received from investors, will show up here. It is possible to also discover information about educational backgrounds, companies the advisor has worked for over the years, types of licensing or registration--depending upon what products are offered--most advisors are likely to be listed on this website. For example, advisors who offer variable annuities must have a securities registration, so it is important to be sure that the advisor has the proper license to conduct securities or insurance business. This can also be checked at www.finra.org/brokercheck to find disciplinary actions taken against brokers and registered representatives. Check www.adviserinfo.sec.gov for registered investment advisor firms and investment advisor representatives with disciplinary actions; look under investment advisor search.

In order to find out about a particular representative, one can locate the representatives Form ADV on the website. The most recent Form ADV for an advisor is located online on the Investment Advisor Public Disclosure (IAPD) website. In addition, a copy of the form can also be obtained from the investment advisor in question, the state securities regulator, or the SEC (this will depend upon the size of the advisory firm). There are two parts to this form. The first part of this form provides information about the advisor's business and whether or not the advisor has had any issues with either clients or regulators. The second part of the Form ADV provides the minimum requirements for a written disclosure statement, which is typically referred to as "the brochure." This is what advisors need to provide to prospective clients upfront before conducting any business, as well as to existing clients each year.

This brochure describes how the advisor's practice operates, as well as gives details about fees, and whether or not the advisor has any conflicts of interest. Each brochure that is offered to customers must also include a brochure supplement that provides information regarding any persons who act on behalf of that advisor, in terms of providing investment advice and interacting with customers. This brochure must be given to customers before the investment representative gives any investment advice in a client relationship.

After having obtained information on the registration and records of a financial advisor or a firm, it is important to also know about investor protections if one plans to move forward and place some or all assets with an advisor. For example, find out if the firm, as well as its clearing firm, is a member of the Securities Investor Protection Corporation (SIPC). The Securities Investor Protection Corporation provides some customer protection if a brokerage firm becomes insolvent or commits fraud. However, it is important to note that the SIPC does not insure against losses that are a result of a market decline. In addition, individuals will typically not be covered if the investor has placed funds with a non-SIPC member or if the financial firm goes out of business.

Avoiding Scams

There are many scams in the financial services industry and unfortunately, many individuals become victims to these frauds and lose some – or even all of their savings every year. The SEC offers advice on how to avoid scams and here are some of the things that investors can do to help in preventing scams.

Ask questions and then verify the answers to those questions. Many scam artists will rely on the fact that a great many people simply do not follow up or investigate important information prior to placing money in an investment or other financial opportunity. It is simply not enough to ask the advisor for more information, as it would only be more of the same fraudulent "facts." Instead, check out the information from other sources, verify first, then consider trust. Take some time to really research the investments and other products that are being offered in order to make sure they are what the advisor has said they are.

It may also help to research other companies before investing with one in particular. Prior to investing in a company's stock or other opportunity, one should fully understand the company's business and its products or services. Before purchasing any shares of stock in particular, be sure to read over the company's financial statements on the SEC's website. It is possible to also contact each states securities regulator. Most companies are required to file financial statements with the SEC and states they are doing business in.

Know the advisor. As mentioned, spend some time doing research on any financial services representative before doing any investment of any money at all. This includes finding out if the advisor is correctly licensed and if the advisor or the firm has had any disciplinary issues with regulators or clients.

Be skeptical about solicited offers. Should one receive a call or an email from an advisor out of the blue regarding any type of investment, be sure to research both the advisor and the investment opportunity offered.

Remember, if it sounds too good to be true, it probably is. Compare any promised returns with actual current, recent or past returns on the investment recommended.

There is no such thing as a guaranteed return in securities, so be careful. Even the safest of investments or financial opportunities carries with it some degree of risk. Typically, this will correlate with the return that can be expected on the investment. In other words, if money truly is perfectly safe, then it will likely generate a lower return. Likewise, just the opposite is true as well; if high returns are likely, there is probably going to be a great deal of risk involved, too.

Pretty marketing materials do not mean that a firm or advisor is legitimate. Pretty websites and brochures are fairly easy to make in this day and age. In fact, a nice looking simple website can be created in just a few hours. Therefore, just because a company or advisor has nice-looking marketing materials, it does not mean that a legitimate financial opportunity is being offered.

Do not cave in to pressure to invest immediately or miss a "great opportunity." Scam artists will often tell victims about a limited-onetime-only opportunity and that if an investment isn't made immediately, the client will lose out forever. Here again, research the "opportunity" prior to investing any money or just simply pass.

In any case, being an educated investor or consumer is the best defense against scams. So take the time to do homework before putting money anywhere. It will be more than worth the effort to do so.

Other Sources for Investor Education and Safety

It seems that every year, con artists and scammers become more and more sophisticated with ways to con consumers and investors out of hard-earned assets.

Since investor and consumer education awareness are the first line of defense against fraud and scams, there are several organizations whose focus is on helping to prevent such activities.

In addition to the SEC and FINRA, there are other good resources for individuals and investors to check the background of advisors, as well as to find other helpful resources on investing safely while avoiding fraud. Check out the; *National Ethics association (NEA), Local Better Business Bureaus (BBB),* and many others including the *North American Securities Administrators Association (NASAA).*

The North American Securities Administrators Association, or NASAA, is the oldest international organization that is focused on protecting investors. The NASAA has members in all fifty states of the United States, as well as in Puerto Rico, Canada, Mexico, and the U.S. Virgin Islands. This organization's members share the common goal of protecting investors and consumers from the many types of financial fraud that befall consumers and even some experienced investors.

In the U.S., this organization is primarily responsible for efficient capital formation and grassroots investor protection, primarily focusing on those consumers who are involved in purchasing advice on investments and securities. Members of NASAA participate in enforcement actions as well as in sharing information. In addition, the organization coordinates and implements training and education seminars each year for securities agency staff.

There are many ways that NASAA members work within each state's government in helping to protect consumer investors as well as helping in maintaining the integrity of the securities industry. Some of these include:

- Registering various securities that are offered to investors in particular states;
- Enforcing state securities laws;
- Licensing investment advisor and securities firms, as well as stockbrokers;
- Investigating complaints from investors as well as cases of alleged investment fraud;
- Reviewing various securities offerings that may not be exempt from state law;
- Educating investors regarding his or her rights;
- Providing tools for investor assistance in investment decision making;
- Examining brokerage and investment advisor firms to ensure compliance;
- Advocating the passage of positive securities regulations and laws;

NASAA also has posted some tips for consumers on how to spot a con artist in the financial services field. Knowing these tips can help one avoid placing his or her money in the wrong hands.

Recognizing Scammers

Scammers try to blend in. In trying to disguise their true motives, these con artists do their best to look and sound familiar and very relaxed. These scammers will also try to blend in with various groups within the community and will therefore quickly get to know lots of people in the group so as to help push "referrals" and spread information about "investments." Ironically this is also the way many legitimate advisors also become known and trusted!

Con artists dress well. These scammers also try to give off a look of success and will act and dress very professionally to seem successful. They may even work from a very nice office space in order to impress prospective clients--again the same as solid trustworthy advisors.

Scammers typically push poorly understood products. With so many different financial products on the market today, it is easy for people to get confused. This actually plays into the con artist's plan perfectly, as to not seem so suspect if offering products that are confusing to understand and "difficult to explain."

Those involved in frauds will bring out the worst in individuals as prospective clients. Oftentimes con artists are able to exploit negative traits in victims, such as fear or greed. Fear will come out when the scammer tries to convince the victim that one will be spoiling the investment for others if the authorities were alerted. In fact, unlike trained financial advisors who welcome questions to help clients understand, con artists will try to make others feel inadequate if too many questions are asked. One key here is not to let emotions rule and lead one into a bad investment based on a scam.

Con artists promote products that seem too good to be true. Even though all investments involve some degree of risk, con artists stress that their product is absolutely the greatest... that losing money is next to impossible or that the great tip came from an inside source, please, run the other way!

However, verifiable bank and insurance regulated financial products may be correctly explained as safe and secure financial strategies or products.

Con artists can seem very friendly. In fact, one may seem like the perfect financial advisor by taking a personal interest in the client, returning phone calls promptly, and basically doing everything that should be done. However, once someone has made an investment with the scammer, the phone calls suddenly stop and the friendliness can fade beyond recognition.

Con artists don't always ask the best questions. One should also be aware of when a financial advisor does not ask questions regarding past investment experience, or tolerance to risk, or any other pertinent information that one would need in order to make an appropriate or suitable recommendation, this may be a sign of questionable, inept, or fraudulent activity.

Once determined that the advisor is not legitimate, there are a few things that can be done to protect one's self as well as others. Avoid becoming a victim, contact the state securities regulator and report any suspicions. The state securities or insurance department will be able to tell one if the individual advisor is even licensed, and if he or she has run into any disciplinary issues in the past. In addition, contact the local Better Business Bureau office. They can inform as to whether there have been any other consumer complaints registered about the advisor that is being considered.

American Association of Retired Persons (AARP)

The American Association of Retired Persons or AARP also helps in providing important information to investors and consumers of financial products and on how to best protect themselves from fraud and scams.

AARP helps those who are considering working with a financial advisor by offering a financial advisor questionnaire that helps individuals, especially retirees and those approaching retirement, in knowing what to ask before placing trust and money with a financial services representative. Be aware though that AARP has conflicts of interest since they too sell investments, advice, and insurance products for profit.

These questions include requests for information about licensure and registration of advisors as well as the firms the advisor may be affiliated with. They also include asking for details on whether a broker or advisor has been disciplined either by regulators or by a professional ethics organization.

In addition, it is suggested that consumers and potential investors ask an advisor for a letter of engagement that spells out the services that the client will receive, as well as the role and responsibilities of the advisor and the type of advisor compensation that will be expected.

In addition to the information needed prior to establishing a relationship with a financial advisor, AARP suggests that one should ask for a regular assessment, after becoming a client, of a financial portfolio's progress from the tax professional that handles the advisory client's tax return as a confidential double-check on the advisors results and professional skill level.

AARP also suggests that individuals considering an advisor should speak with current clients about whether the advisor has provided good and timely communication; and find out if there have been any recent changes in staff at the advisors financial services firm affecting customer service levels in any negative way. In addition, ask some of the advisors clients if the growth of their portfolios has matched expectations based on the advisor's original projections.

Video: <u>Is it Crazy or Smart to Work with an Internet Specialist</u>

<u>Click & Watch this video to learn more...</u>

Video URL: <u>http://annuityguys.com/give-money-to-an-annuity-specialist-on-the-internet-are-you-crazy</u>

QR Code for smart phones:

Chapter 13: Some Annuities Are Ugly!

"*Beware of ignorance, wrong motives, and misinformation that produce thinly veiled self-serving recommendations.*

Truth shall prevail!" - Anonymous

UGLY Annuities

It is a fact that many annuities are horrible financial vehicles, just like many mutual funds, stocks, bonds, ETFs, banking instruments, and scores of alternative derivative securities have wrecked many portfolios including some entire retiree's futures.

The alternative is to bury money in the backyard and avoid any chance of making a bad decision, or to realize that there are also annuities and securities that are excellent financial vehicles to enhance growth, income, and a secure retirement. Remember that money in the backyard is at risk of inflationary devaluation and hostile un-neighborly acquisition!

Annuities are frequently oversold and overstated by unqualified commission-focused salespeople, or unfairly criticized by a biased investment industry that wants money to stay at risk where it produces ongoing residual income for the investment advisor, brokerage firm and/or the broker.

The truth lies somewhere in the middle. As one reads the article reprinted below, it can actually be applied in some way to all types of annuities, not just fixed index- or hybrid-annuities.

The key to success is solid research and working with a professional who has training and experience to assist in structuring financial instruments that have truly stood the test of time and that are prioritized to meet financial and retirement objectives of a particular individual.

Market Free™ Annuities Unfairly Attacked

TV viewers may have seen the NBC Dateline report aired back in April 2008, about insurance agents selling equity index annuities (EIA) which are not equities at all. In fact, they are actually just a Market Free™ fixed annuity with an index option (FIA) which will allow higher interest growth potential. EIAs/FIAs and annuities in general have been regularly criticized and attacked, which in all fairness, is mostly unwarranted wrong spirited bias. A couple of contributing factors are:

1) *An unqualified or at times an unethical insurance salesman*. Far too often, some advisors who offer EIAs/FIAs to retirees are inadequately trained resulting in incompetence and sometimes simply deceitful sales tactics, not accurately explaining the annuity's advantages and disadvantages or the retirement pros and cons involved with owning annuities.

Remember: Time tested dedicated financial experts are quite different from an un-qualified self serving insurance agent. A true and proven retirement planner will have the references, experience and notoriety to back up his or her licensure and credentials. Reputable agents and advisors can be checked out and verified by client references, background reports,

Better Business Bureau reports and editorial authorship of various educational contributions made available for public scrutiny (websites, editorial press, articles or quotes in periodicals, authored books, & etc.).

It's important to note that there are some very competent financial advisors primarily in the insurance industry. They have progressed from a starting point and acquired the necessary education and experience. They have demonstrated an understanding when offering current, sophisticated retirement planning using advanced annuity strategies. Check credentials and more importantly experience; also do background checks. It should always be an advantage to work with a true professional.

2) *Overzealous insurance advisors overstating performance.* Fixed index annuities are like any other financial vehicle--if used properly, they work great; if used in unsuitable ways, it can be a disappointment and a hindrance to reaching retirement goals.

Unfortunately, annuities are misrepresented too often--with statements like *"full market returns with no risk."* The no risk to principal is true, and at times they do equal or beat the market indices. However, that is not always true. In a strong economy with stocks doing well, it is expected that the fixed index annuity will fall several percentage points behind the market return. FIAs with a 3 to 5 percent interest return and no risk to principal would be considered a win-win situation for many retirement plans-- so, overstating performance never helps prospective clients it only sets the stage for disappointment giving a great financial instrument an undeserved black-eye.

FIAs are annuity contracts between the client and a life insurance company. They are simply fixed annuities with an option to be linked to the performance of a stock market or commodity index, commonly but not limited to the S&P 500, Dow Jones Industrials, or the NASDAQ. FIAs have a guaranteed minimum rate of return (guaranteed by the insurance company, not the FDIC) and it gives the ability to capture a portion of index gains with no market losses. That's the upside. Overall, FIAs are not designed to beat the stock market, yet according to a 2010 Wharton study it found that many FIA's have outperformed major stock indexes from 1999 through 2010. They are basically designed to outperform the fixed financial products such as bank CDs, money markets, and higher quality bonds.

One downside is that individuals usually have to hold onto a fixed index annuity for several years to enjoy its full advantage. The term to maturity is typically eight to twelve years, and sometimes longer. An individual who has placed money in an annuity cannot just go and pull funds out like one can with a money market or savings account. If individuals do need to withdraw money from an FIA soon after signing the contract, the following may apply:

- A surrender charge may be owed. It varies from annuity to annuity, but it can be in the vicinity of 9 to 12 percent of the initial principal/premium.
- Most FIAs allow 10 percent annual withdrawals with no penalty.
- Some or all of the index-linked interest may be lost for a specific time period that the FIA has yet to lock-in on the portion withdrawn.
- Tax may be owed only on the increase in value of the annuity. (Withdrawals taken before age fifty-nine and a half may be subject to a 10 percent tax penalty on earnings.)

It is important to plan properly so the fixed index annuity can be a long-term solution for individual retirement needs. It is possible to lose money if one should need to fully surrender an FIA soon after opening it. This should rarely or never happen with proper planning.

For instance when an individual chooses to keep money liquid and thus make 4 percent instead of the opportunity to make 6 percent interest per year, one will actually pay a lost opportunity penalty of 31 percent by default. That extra compounded 2 percent lost could have increased the asset value by 31 percent, at 6 percent interest rather than 4 percent. Thus, keeping money unnecessarily liquid that could have earned a couple of extra percentage points of interest over ten years may cost by default three hundred percent more than the cost of a potential surrender charge--full surrenders via negative bias are often overstated, fear-mongered, and ironically with proper planning--rarely experienced!

So, if one plans well, the fixed index annuity has the potential to make a significant difference over fixed investments, cash equivalents, and, at times, it actually can beat the stock market!

This attack on annuities could be about variable, fixed, immediate, hybrid, or any other type of annuity. The moral to this story is get good advice while doing one's own due diligence, and realize that bad advisors and annuities exist; while good advisors and good annuities will prevail, as they have stood and will continue to stand the test of time.

Video: <u>The Too Good to Be True 8 Percent Annuity Return Secret</u>

<u>Click & Watch this video to understand more about the secret...</u>

Video URL: http://annuityguys.com/is-the-8-percent-annuity-secret-to-good-to-be-true

QR Code for smart phones:

Chapter 14: Is Social Security an Annuity?

"I should have listened to my nieces and nephews when they told me to stop spending money faster than they were giving it to me"

"The mint makes it first, it is up to you to make it last."

- Evan Esar

Should Social Security be Relied On?

Before we discuss the complexities and facts about using Social Security to its fullest extent as an integral, and for some a primary, component in one's retirement plan, it is important to cut through the hyperbole. Getting down to the facts surrounding the political and financial reality of Social Security's probability of remaining viable is important for those nearing or already in retirement.

Negative Press Gets Attention

Everywhere one turns, there are headlines stating that Social Security is doomed and that relying on it is foolhardy--looking deeper into its true viability at least for those now retired and for most of the baby boomers moving into retirement--it is likely to remain and continue pretty close to the way it was designed and it should remain viable.

There has been a constant bombardment of negative press for years about Social Security's demise; to the point where many retirees have decided inadvertently by lack of attention and inaction, to ignore or overlook it as a reliable component of retirement. The truth is that Social Security, for the majority of retirees, is an integral part, if not the most substantial portion of their overall retirement income. Unfortunately as a result of all the negative press, too many retirees believe social security may not be around for long and have become complacent about how to best structure what may well be one of their largest cash flow assets.

Ignoring Social Security by taking it early or at full retirement age (FAR) without understanding the best ways to optimize, can be a huge mistake that can cost a married couple well over one hundred thousand dollars in lost retirement income based on today's dollars and much more when we consider the future value of this benefit.

It is true that we are in trouble as a country, if we do not correct the excesses and abuses of government spending to get our fiscal house in order.

Not only is this necessary to save Social Security but for every government service or program we rely on or they will all cease to exist, as we know them now. Is this a likely scenario? In the opinion of this author, no spelled *"NO"* however, do I see a rocky road ahead with some cutbacks? The answer is *"YES,"* in all capitals!

We are a nation that has overcome what would seem to be insurmountable obstacles, time and again, to become the envy of the world in terms of financial superiority, military might, and personal liberties. It is the combination of our constitution, free enterprise system, legislative process, and the sheer ingenuity of the American people that gives us the ability to conquer any problem and succeed. Like it or not Social Security has been woven into the fabric of our society. It is likely that answers to a balanced approach will be found that keep Social Security viable. We the people will get our fiscal house in order one way or another.

So, take Social Security seriously; citizens have contributed to it, use it, optimize it, and for most Americans it will be a substantial component of retirement income planning.

Social Security's Impact On US Citizens

What did retirees do before 1935 when Social Security was not available? What about those less fortunate who had no supplement for their retirement income to survive?

Before Social Security, there was more family and church involvement on behalf of the poor--surviving hardships. Here are some recent statistics from www.SSA.gov that demonstrate why Social Security, like it or not, is likely to be continued to a large degree as part of what it means to be a Social Security entitled US citizen.

- In 2011, nearly 55 million Americans will receive $727 billion in Social Security benefits.
- Social Security is the major source of income for most of the elderly.
- Nine out of ten individuals age 65 and older receive Social Security benefits.

- Social Security benefits represent about 41% of the income of the elderly.
- Among elderly Social Security beneficiaries, 54% of married couples and 73% of unmarried persons receive 50% or more of their income from Social Security.
- Among elderly Social Security beneficiaries, 22% of married couples and about 43% of unmarried persons rely on Social Security for 90% or more of their income.
- Social Security provides more than just retirement benefits.
- Retired workers and their dependents account for 69% of total benefits paid.
- Disabled workers and their dependents account for 19% of total benefits paid.
- Just over 1 in 4 of today's 20 year-olds will become disabled before reaching age 67.
- 67% of the private sector workforce has no long-term disability insurance.
- Survivors of deceased workers account for about 12% of total benefits paid.
- About 1 in 8 of today's 20 year-olds will die before reaching age 67.
- About 97% of persons aged 20-49 who worked in covered employment in 2010 have survivor's insurance protection for their young children and the surviving spouse caring for the children.
- An estimated 158 million workers, 94% of all workers are covered under Social Security.
- 50% of the workforce has no private pension coverage.
- 31% of the workforce has no savings set aside specifically for retirement.
- In 1940, the life expectancy of a 65-year-old was almost 14 years; today it's almost 20 years.
- By 2036, there will be almost twice as many older Americans as today -- from 41.9 million today to 78.1 million.
- There are currently 2.9 workers for each Social Security beneficiary. By 2036, there will be 2.1 workers for each beneficiary.

Is Social Security the Ultimate Annuity?

It is important to understand the way that Social Security was designed to function. By commercial standards, this is the ultimate lifetime annuity. The definition of an annuity is basically exchanging one's money with some entity in return for a reliable income stream over a period of time, based on a pre-determined agreement. The strength of the annuity in this case is the full backing of the US government which is considered to be the safest financial haven of the entire world. The primary reason it is not an annuity is that it is not contractually guaranteed and can be legislated away partially or in full! With this being said, Social Security's ultimate annuity aspects are:

- Full Backing of the US Government;
- Tax advantaged - 0 to 85 percent is taxed based on income;
- Inflation Protection - cost of living increases (COLAS) ;
- Income for life - eliminating longevity risk;
- Spousal, Family and Survivor benefits;
- Priced less than commercially available annuities.

Understanding Social Security

With so many misnomers about Social Security, here are some interesting factors:

1. Passed by Congress in 1935 and signed into law by President Franklin D. Roosevelt;

2. In 1956, it was amended to include disabilities;

3. Eligibility and benefit payout is gender neutral;

4. Additional income earning at full retirement age (FRA) is allowed with no reduction in benefit;

5. Earning additional income after election at an early retirement age (ERA) is allowed with some reduction in benefit. Benefits reduced by earnings increase future benefits;

6. Same sex marriage partners do not qualify for spousal benefits since they fail the definition of marriage under *"The Defense of Marriage Act"*;

7. Social Security benefits are officially referred to as "Old Age Benefits";

8. The retirement income benefit (RIB) is calculated from the primary insurance amount (PIA);

- 35 years of the retiree's highest earnings are added and averaged using an average index monthly earnings (AIME) formula in determining his or her PIA.
- PIA is based on several factors and is calculated to allow enrollment at FRA to receive the full RIB.

9. Social Security is taxed based on predetermined income levels.

- A portion of a retirement income benefit may be taxable based on Provisional Income.
- Single Social Security; Taxed Portion 2010 Percentages
  Up to $25,000 is 0%; $25,000 to $34,000 is 50%; $34,001+ is 85%
- Joint Social Security; Taxed Portion 2010 Percentages
  Up to $32,000 is 0%; $32,000 to $44,000 is 50%; $44,001+ is 85%

10. Age 62 is considered the beginning of one's early retirement age (ERA). One must accept a discounted or lower retirement income benefit (RIB) for starting benefits early;

11. Age 65 to 67, depending on when one was born, is considered full retirement age (FRA). This is the age where the RIB is paid in full with no discount to the PIA;

12. Early retirement age (ERA) income benefits at 62, for those born between 1943 and 1954 are reduced by about 25 percent based on the PIA at FRA. Spousal benefits are reduced even more by about 30 percent;

13. Being deemed at an early retirement age signifies that one has been deemed to have received all of the benefits available in one's month of entitlement;

14. Delayed retirement credits are earned when income is delayed beyond FRA. The annual credit is based on approximately 8 percent simple interest or monthly interest of .0066667 percent;

15. A restricted application can be filed after FRA for a married couple to claim a spousal benefit while continuing to receive delayed retirement credits;

16. File and suspend is a strategy that can be used to receive delayed retirement credits this also allows an eligible spouse to make a spousal claim;

- One, file and suspend strategy (of which there are many) is for spouse one at FRA to file and suspend, allowing spouse two to claim a spousal benefit. This allows spouse two to receive substantial income while spouse one can grow his or her income benefit with delayed credits.

- Cross claiming is not allowed where both spouses receive spousal benefits with or without restricted applications simultaneously.

17. Switching between strategies and using different eligibility ages creates a multitude of possible family benefit (couples) outcomes;

18. The Social Security Administration offers mostly simple calculators that are based on an individuals' eligibility age and earnings history. They have a quite limited ability when it comes to comparing the multitude of more complex scenarios;

- Social Security employees do not typically give advanced planning advice but do offer retirement income benefit information for individuals based mostly on eligibility, age and past earnings history.

19. Individuals are allowed to receive their retirement income benefit based on their own earnings record or up to 50 percent of the higher earning spouse's PIA, if it calculates to a higher retirement income benefit less any reductions for claiming at an early retirement age;

- This calculation is sometimes explained as topping off or topping up.

- Topping off or up is actually receiving the lower earning spouse's retirement income benefit and then topping it off or up with the higher earning spouse's PIA until it reaches half of the higher earning spouses PIA.

20. Spousal survivor's retirement income benefit can begin as early as age 60 (and age 50 if disabled) provided the marriage was not less than nine months and the decedent was eligible. When dependent children are younger than sixteen, the surviving spouse can be eligible at a younger age;

- Taking spousal survivor benefits prior to FRA will discount or reduce retirement benefit income based upon a disproportionately lower rate rather than a discounted PIA based on an individual's own earnings record and PIA.

21. Un-remarried divorcees are entitled to survivor benefits if they were married for 10 years or more during the decedent's lifetime;

22. The Windfall Elimination Provision (WEP) may reduce but not eliminate benefits for individuals with pensions that were earned outside of the Social Security System depending on multiple factors such as earnings record, years of social security credits and age of eligibility;

23. Government Pension Offset (GPO) - when one earns a government pension not based on Social Security, it is likely to reduce spousal or survivor benefits by two-thirds and can be reduced to zero;

24. It is possible to start over with an election decision within a twelve month period in the event one feels that a mistake was made. To do this, one must fill out a form and payback all benefits received.

Summary

Those that understand the importance of optimizing Social Security will inevitably need some outside planning help. The Social Security Administration offers little guidance in the area of optimization other than giving income payouts based on the retirees' earnings record and a proposed start date with no maximization analysis of the family benefit. The vast majority of advisors do not offer social security planning and are ill equipped, so generic advice is given instead of actually knowing what's best.

Comprehensive Social Security planning takes a specialist --having the proper analytical software combined with experience and the knowledge to design cash flow strategies in retirement that can produce optimum results. This type of expert can be scarce and in more demand than a general advisor or broker, so one may have to search more diligently to find this type of retirement planning advisor. They should be able to help with not just the Social Security aspect but also the cash flow analysis to weave the entirety of a successful retirement income and estate plan together. Using available assets and income streams for income at optimal time periods will achieve a retirees' most optimized total cash flow in retirement considering all factors.

Social Security optimization is not intended to be a stand-alone income stream or calculation rather it is an integral portion of one's overall retirement income planning.

Video: <u>Social Security is it Considered to be the Ultimate Annuity?</u>

<u>Click & Watch this video to understand how Social Security is an integral part of most retirement income plans...</u>

Video URL: http://annuityguys.com/social-security-and-income-planning

QR Code for smart phones:

Dear Reader,

We hope you enjoyed this book and benefit by having a better understanding of how annuities may fit into your retirement plan.

Again Best Wishes on your Successful Retirement!

Dick & Eric, Annuity Guys

Retirement Educators

If you have benefited from this annuity reference book please make others aware by giving your opinion in a review at Amazon.com.

Please send an email to retirewell@dvdfinancial.com if you have any questions or suggestions for how this book might be improved.

Annuity/Financial Glossary

1035 Exchange - Section 1035 sets out provisions for the exchange of similar (insurance-related) assets without any tax consequences upon the conversion. If the exchange qualifies for like-kind exchange consideration, income taxes are deferred until the new property or asset is sold. The 1035 exchange provisions are only available for a limited type of asset, which includes cash value life insurance policies and annuity contracts.

401(k) Plan - A 401(k) plan is a tax-deferred contribution retirement plan that gives eligible employees the opportunity to defer a portion of his or her current compensation into the plan. Amounts that are deferred are excluded from the participant's gross income for the year of the deferral. The plan may provide for employer matching contributions and discretionary profit-sharing contributions.

403(b) Plan - A tax-deferred retirement plan that is available to employees of public schools and colleges, and certain non-profit hospitals, charitable, religious, scientific, and educational organizations.

457 Plan - A type of non-qualified deferred compensation plan that is available to employees of state and local governments and tax-exempt organizations.

Accelerated Death Benefits - Some life insurance policies make a portion of the death benefit available prior to the death of the insured. Such benefits are usually available only due to terminal illness or for long-term care situations.

Accidental Death Benefit - An accidental death benefit is a rider that is added to an insurance policy, which provides that an additional death benefit will be paid in the event death is caused by an accident. This rider is often called double indemnity.

Accumulation Phase - The time period when the annuity holder is able to fund the annuity by making one lump sum deposit or a series of deposits over time.

Annuitant – The individual who purchases an annuity and is entitled to receive its benefits.

Annuitization - The time when the annuity is converted from an account that is accumulating money to an account that pays out an income stream.

Annuitization Phase – The time period when the annuity holder is receiving the annuity's benefits.

Annuity - A contract between an insurance company and an individual, which generally guarantees lifetime income to the individual on whose life the contract is based in return for either a lump sum or periodic payment to the insurance company. Interest earned inside of an annuity is income-tax-deferred until it is paid out or withdrawn.

Appreciation – Appreciation is the increase in value of an asset. The term appreciation may be applied to real estate, stocks, bonds, etc.

Ask Price – The price at which a seller is willing to sell a security or commodity.

Bankruptcy - A federal court proceeding in which a debtor who is unable to continue to meet his or her financial obligations may be relieved from the payment of certain debts. This action seriously affects the borrower's creditworthiness.

Basis – An amount usually representing the actual cost of an investment to the buyer. The basis amount of an investment is important in calculating capital gains and losses, depreciation, and other income tax calculations.

Basis Points – Basis points is a term used by investment professionals to describe yields of bonds. One basis point equals one one-hundredth of 1 percent, or 0.01 percent. A bond yield increase from 10.0 percent to 10.1 percent represents an increase of ten basis points.

Bear Market – A prolonged decline in overall stock prices occurring over a period of months or even years.

Beneficiary – The person who is designated to receive the benefits of a contract.

Beta - A statistically generated number that is used to measure the volatility of a security or mutual fund in comparison to the market as a whole.

Bid Price - The price that a buyer is willing to pay for a security or commodity.

Blue Chip Stocks - The equity issues of financially stable, well-established companies that usually have a history of being able to pay dividends in bear and bull markets.

Bond - A certificate of indebtedness issued by a government entity or a corporation which pays a fixed cash coupon at regular intervals. The coupon payment is normally a fixed percentage of the initial investment. The face value of the bond is repaid to the investor upon maturity.

Bonus Annuity - Certain annuities that have surrender charges will offer rewards to investors by offering a type of bonus. For example, the annuity holder may be able to withdraw a certain percentage of his or her premium payments per year without being penalized. The tradeoff for offering the bonus is typically that the annuity will then have a longer length of surrender period.

Book Value - The value that belongs to a company's owners or shareholders after total liabilities have been subtracted from total assets; also called shareholders' equity.

Bull Market - A prolonged increase in overall stock prices, usually occurring over a period of months or even years.

Buy-Down - The payment of additional discount points in return for a below-market interest rate (and therefore a lower monthly payment) on a home mortgage.

Buy-Sell Agreement - An agreement between shareholders or business partners to purchase each other's shares in specified circumstances.

CD-type Annuity - A hybrid between a fixed annuity and a certificate of deposit (CD). These annuities guarantee a fixed rate of return throughout the entire duration of the annuity contract, typically anywhere between one and ten years. Rates will vary depending upon the issuing insurance company.

Capital Markets - A general term encompassing all markets for financial instruments with more than one year to maturity.

Capital Stock - All ownership shares of a company, both common and preferred, listed at par value.

Cash Equivalents - Assets that can be quickly converted to cash. These include receivables, treasury bills, short-term commercial paper, short-term municipal corporate bonds and notes.

Cash Value - Permanent life insurance policies provide both a death benefit and an investment component called a cash value. The cash value earns interest and often appreciates. The policyholder may accumulate significant cash value over the years and, in some circumstances, "borrow" the appreciated funds without paying taxes on the borrowed gains. As long as the policy stays in force, the borrowed funds do not need to be repaid, but interest may be charged to the cash value account.

Certificate of Deposit (CD) - A low-risk, often federally guaranteed, investment offered by banks. A CD pays interest to investors for as long as five years. The interest rate on a CD is fixed for the duration of the CD term.

Charitable Remainder Trust (CRT) - An irrevocable trust with both charitable and non-charitable beneficiaries. The donor transfers highly appreciated assets into the trust and retain an income interest. Upon expiration of the income interest, the remainder in the trust passes to a qualified charity of the donor's choice. If properly structured, the CRT permits the donor to receive income, estate, or gift tax advantages, or all three. These advantages often provide for a much greater income stream to the income beneficiary than would be available outside the trust.

Closed-End Fund - A fund whose value is held within a fixed number of shares. Shares can be bought and sold on the stock exchange or the over-the-counter market.

Codicil - An instrument in writing executed by a testator for adding to, altering, explaining, or confirming a will previously made by the testator. This is executed with the same formalities as a will and also has the effect of bringing the date of the will forward to the date of codicil.

Collateral - Assets pledged as security for a loan. If the borrower defaults on payment, the lender may dispose of the property pledged as security to raise money to repay the loan.

Commission - The fee a broker or insurance agent collects for administering a trade or policy.

Commodity - A physical substance such as a food or a metal that investors buy or sell on a commodities exchange, usually via futures contracts.

Common Stock - A security that represents ownership in a corporation.

Compounding - The computation of interest paid using the principal plus the previously earned interest.

Conduit IRA - An individual who rolled over a total distribution from a qualified plan into an IRA can later roll over those assets into a new employer's plan. In this case, the IRA has been used as a holding account, or a conduit.

Consumer Debt - Debt incurred for consumable or depreciating non-investment assets. Items include credit card debt, store-financed consumer purchases, car loans, and family loans that will be repaid.

Contrarian - An individual whose opinion is the opposite of the majority.

Convertible Term Insurance - Term life insurance that can be converted to a permanent or whole-life policy without evidence of insurability, subject to time limitations.

Corporation - A legal business entity created under state law. Because the corporation is a separate entity from its owners, shareholders have no legal liability for its debts.

Correction - A sudden decline in stock or bond prices after a period of market strength.

Coupon Rate - The rate of interest paid on a bond, expressed as a percentage of the bond's par value.

Critical Illness Insurance - Insurance protection designed to provide a lump sum payment equal to the full value of the policy or a percentage of the policy, depending upon the product design, to the insured or policy owner upon the diagnosis of a covered critical illness. Typical illnesses covered include heart attack, stroke, cancer, paralysis, renal failure, and Alzheimer's disease. Many policies offer a partial payment for certain medical procedures such as coronary bypass surgery or angioplasty. Some policies offer a return of all premiums in the event of death of the insured, while others pay the full benefit upon the insured's death.

Currency Risk - The level of risk when investing in international markets, due to the fluctuations in exchange rates of the various world currencies. Investing in any foreign country should be preceded by a careful estimation of how well its currency is likely to do against the dollar.

Custodian - A financial institution, usually a bank or trust company that holds a person's or company's cash or securities in safekeeping.

Cyclical Companies - Companies that report strong earnings when the overall economy is doing well and weaker earnings when the economy is in recession.

Death Benefit Provision - The funds that are paid out to a beneficiary should the annuity owner pass away. This amount is typically the amount of the account balance and possibly an additional insurance benefit.

Debt Markets - The fixed income sector of the capital markets devoted to trading debt securities issued by corporations and governments.

Decedent - A person who has died.

Decreasing Term - A term life insurance policy featuring a decreasing death benefit. Decreasing term is well suited to provide for an obligation that decreases over the years, such as a mortgage.

Deferral - A form of tax sheltering in which all earnings are allowed to compound tax-free until they are withdrawn at a future date. Placing funds in a qualified plan, for example, triggers deductions for the current tax year (in most cases) and postpones capital gains or other income taxes until the funds are withdrawn from the plan.

Deferred Compensation - Income withheld by an employer and paid at some future time, usually upon retirement or termination of employment.

Deferred Payout - When annuity payments begin at a time in the future rather than beginning immediately upon funding the annuity.

Defined Benefit Plan - A defined benefit plan pays participants a specific retirement benefit that is promised (defined) in the plan document. Under a defined benefit plan, benefits must be definitely determinable. For example, a plan that entitles a participant to a monthly pension benefit for life equal to 30 percent of monthly compensation is a defined benefit plan.

Defined Contribution Plan - In a defined contribution plan, contributions are allocated to individual accounts according to a predetermined contribution allocation. This type of plan does not promise any specific dollar benefit to a participant at retirement. Benefits received are based on amounts contributed, investment performance, and vesting. The most common type of defined contribution plan is the 401(k) profit-sharing plan.

Deflation - A period in which the general price level of goods and services is declining.

Depreciation - Charges made against earnings to write off the cost of a fixed asset over its estimated useful life. Depreciation does not represent a cash outlay. It is a bookkeeping entry representing the decline in value of an asset over time.

Direct Deposit - A means of authorizing payment made by governments or companies to be deposited directly into a recipient's account. Used mainly for the deposit of salary, pension, and interest checks.

Disability Insurance - Insurance designed to replace a percentage of earned income if accident or illness prevents the beneficiary from pursuing his or her livelihood.

Disposable Income - After-tax income available for spending, saving, or investing.

Distribution Phase - The time period over which the annuity pays out income benefits. These payments may be either fixed or variable.

Diversification - Spreading investment risk among a number of different securities, properties, companies, industries, or geographical locations. Diversification does not ensure against market loss.

Dividends - A distribution of the earnings of a company to its shareholders. Dividends are "declared" by the company based on profitability and can change from time to time. There is a direct relationship between dividends paid and share-value growth. The most aggressive growth companies do not pay dividends, and the highest dividend paying companies may not experience dramatic growth.

Dollar Cost Averaging - Buying a mutual fund or securities using a consistent dollar amount of money each month (or other period). More securities will be bought when prices are low, resulting in a lower average cost per share.

Earnings Per Share (EPS) - Total net profits divided by the number of outstanding common shares of a company.

Economic Cycle - Economic events that repeat a regular pattern over a period of anywhere from two to eight years. This pattern of events tends to be slightly different each time but usually has a large number of similarities to previous cycles.

Effective Tax Rate - The percentage of total income paid in federal and state income taxes.

Efficient Market - The market in which all the available information has been analyzed and is reflected in the current stock price.

Employee Stock Ownership Plans (ESOP) - An ESOP plan allows employees to purchase stock, usually at a discount, that they can hold or sell. ESOPs offer a tax advantage for both employer and employee. The employer earns a tax deduction for contributions of stock or cash used to purchase stock for the employee. The employee pays no tax on these contributions until they are distributed.

Equity-Indexed Annuity - This type of annuity has its returns based on the performance of an underlying equity market index. The principal in the annuity account is protected from losses in the market; however, the gains will be added to the annuity's returns.

Equity-Indexed Deferred Annuity - This is an equity-indexed annuity in which the income benefit payments do not begin until a set time in the future.

Estate - A decedent's estate is equal to the total value of his or her assets as of the date of death. The estate includes all funds, personal effects, interest in business enterprises, titles to property, real estate, stocks, bonds, and notes receivable.

Estate Planning - The orderly arrangement of one's financial affairs to maximize the value transferred at death to the people and institutions favored by the deceased, with minimum loss of value because of taxes and forced liquidation of assets.

Excess Distributions - An individual may have to pay 15 percent tax on distributions received from qualified plans in excess of $150,000 during a single year. The tax, however, does not apply to distributions due to death, distributions that are rolled over, and distributions of after-tax contributions.

Executor - The person named in a will to manage the estate of the deceased according to the terms of the will.

Face Amount - The face amount stated in a life insurance policy is the amount that will be paid upon death or policy maturity. The face amount of a permanent insurance policy may change with time as the cash value in the policy increases.

Fair Market Value - The price that a buyer and seller can establish in an arms-length transaction of a property or other asset where neither one is compelled to buy or to sell.

Family Trust - An inter vivos trust established with family members as beneficiaries.

Fiduciary - An individual or institution occupying a position of trust. An executor, administrator, or trustee.

Financial Planner - A person who helps clients plan and carry out his or her financial futures.

Fixed Annuity - A type of investment offered by insurance companies that guarantees a stream of fixed payments over the life of the annuity. In this case, the insurance company takes on the investment- risk.

Fixed Deferred Annuity - This annuity has guaranteed payments of a fixed amount that do not begin until a set time in the future.

Fixed Index Annuity - The income payments on this type of annuity are either immediate or deferred. Either way, the payments are linked to either an external equity reference or an equity index. These annuities differ from other types of fixed annuities in the way that interest is credited to the annuity's value. Some types of fixed annuities will only credit interest that is calculated at a rate that is set in the annuity contract, while others will also credit interest at rates that are set from time to time by the issuing insurance company.

Fixed Index Deferred Annuity - This annuity is a fixed index annuity in which the income payments to the annuitant do not begin until a set time in the future.

Fixed Investment - Any investment paying a fixed interest rate, such as a money market account, a certificate of deposit, a bond, a note, or a preferred stock. A fixed investment is the opposite of a variable investment.

Flexible Premium Fixed Annuity - This type of annuity is purchased with varying premium payments. These premium payments may be made at different times and in different amounts (typically with a set minimum amount per premium payment). The income benefits to the annuitant are fixed and thus guaranteed by the insurance company.

Flexible Premium Fixed Deferred Annuity - An annuity investor can make premium payments at different times and in varying amounts (subject to a minimum amount) with this type of annuity. The income benefits will begin at a time in the future, and these payments will be fixed and thus guaranteed by the insurance company.

Flexible Premium Variable Annuity - An annuity with flexibility with regard to both when and how much premium is paid into the contract. The income payments from this variable annuity may fluctuate with regard to underlying market conditions and the underlying investment vehicles.

Flexible Premium Variable Deferred Annuity - With this type of annuity, the frequency of the premium payment can vary, and the amount of the premium may also vary (subject to a minimum amount). The income payments will be made for a set period of time, and they are scheduled to begin at a date in the future.

Fluctuation - A variation in the market price of a security.

Fraternal Annuity - An annuity offered to members of a fraternal organization, such as the Knights of Columbus or other group that is not formed for the sole purpose of purchasing insurance or investments.

Fund Manager - A person who manages the assets of a mutual fund.

Fundamental Analysis - A technique of estimating a stock's future value based on the in-depth study of the stock's underlying financial statements. Fundamental analysis is the opposite of technical analysis.

Future Value - The future worth of a payment, or stream of payments, projected at a given interest rate for a given period of time.

Futures Market - A market in which contracts for future delivery of a commodity are bought and sold.

Gift Annuity - These annuities provide an arrangement in which a charitable organization pays out income to an annuitant (and possibly also the annuitant's spouse) in return for an irrevocable transfer of property or cash.

Grace Period - A period (usually thirty-one days) following each premium due date other than the first due date, during which an overdue premium may be paid and during which all policy provisions remain in force and effect.

Group Insurance - A form of insurance designed to insure classes of persons rather than specific individuals.

Growth Stock - The common equity of a company that consistently grows significantly faster than the economy.

Guaranteed Interest Contract Annuity - This annuity offers a guaranteed minimum interest rate that will be credited by the insurance company throughout the accumulation period of the annuity contract.

Guaranteed Investment Certificate (GIC) - A type of debt security sold to individuals by banks and trust companies. They usually cannot be cashed before the specified redemption date, and pay interest at a fixed rate.

Guarantor - A third party who agrees to repay any outstanding balance on a loan if the borrower fails to do so. A guarantor is responsible for the debt only if the principal debtor defaults on the loan.

Guardian - A person or persons named to care for minor children until they reach the age of majority. A will is the best way to ensure that the person or persons whom the decedent wishes to have care for his or her minor children are legally empowered to do so.

Illiquid - The description of a security for which it is difficult to find a buyer or seller. An illiquid investment is an investment that may be difficult to sell quickly at a price close to its market value. Examples include stock in private unlisted companies, commercial real estate, and limited partnerships.

Illustration - A life insurance illustration, or ledger, is a reference tool used to illustrate how a given life insurance policy underwritten by a specific insurer is expected to perform over a period of years. The insurance illustration assumes that conditions remain unchanged over the period of time that the policy is held.

Immediate Annuity - A type of annuity where one single lump sum premium payment is made. Typically, income payments from this type of annuity begin right away. Immediate annuities are normally purchased after an investor has reached retirement. Immediate annuities may be either fixed or variable. If the annuity is variable, then the amount of the income payments may change over time, depending upon the performance of the underlying investments.

Income Annuity - Either a fixed or a variable annuity that pays the annuity owner an amount of money on a monthly basis. Typically, payments begin as soon as the investor purchases the annuity. The length of time that payments are made can be based either on the lifetime of the annuitant or the lifetime of the annuitant's spouse.

Income Averaging - Income averaging allows individuals who were age fifty before January 1, 1986, to pay tax on a lump sum distribution as though it had been received over a five- or ten-year period rather than all at once. By using income averaging, individuals may be able to pay income tax at a more favorable rate.

Income Stocks - Stocks that have a consistent, stable, above-average dividend yield.

Index Annuity - With this annuity, the underlying funds are based on a statistical indicator, such as an equity market index, that provides a representation of the value of the investments in the account. This type of annuity can be considered a hybrid of both a fixed and a variable annuity. The principal that is deposited into an index annuity is protected from downside losses; however, the gains from the underlying investment performance are added to the return.

Index Deferred Annuity - This type of annuity is an index annuity in which the income benefit payments do not begin until a set time in the future.

Individual Retirement Account (IRA) - A personal savings plan that offers tax advantages to those who set aside money for retirement. Depending on the individual's circumstances, contributions to the IRA may be deductible in whole or in part. Generally, amounts in an IRA, including earnings and gains, are not taxed until distributed to the individual.

Individual Retirement Annuity - These annuities are similar to an IRA (individual retirement account). However, in the case of the annuity, the contract needs to be purchased with some conditions that must be met. For example, an individual retirement annuity must be issued in the name of the annuity owner. In addition, only the annuity owner or surviving beneficiaries are allowed to receive the benefits from the annuity.

Inflation - A term used to describe the economic environment of rising prices and declining purchasing power.

In-force Policy - An in-force policy is simply a valid policy. Generally speaking, a life insurance policy will remain in-force as long as sufficient premiums are paid and for approximately thirty-one days thereafter.

Insurability - Insurability refers to the assessment of the applicant's health and is used to gauge the level of risk the insurer would potentially take by underwriting a policy and, therefore, the premium it must charge.

Insured - A life insurance policy covers the life of one or more insured individuals.

Interest Rate - The simple interest rate attached to the terms of a mortgage or other loan. This rate is applied to the outstanding principal owed in determining the portion of a payment attributable to interest and to principal in any given payment.

Interest Rate Risk - The uncertainty in the direction of interest rates. Changes in interest rates could lead to capital loss or a yield less than that available to other investors, putting at risk the earnings capacity of capital.

Intestate - A term describing the legal status of a person who dies without a will.

Investment Banker - A firm that engages in the origination, underwriting, and distribution of new issues.

Investment Company - A corporation or trust whose primary purpose is to invest the funds of its shareholders.

Investment Considerations - Choosing which investments are right, depending upon a number of factors, including an investor's primary objectives, time horizon, and risk tolerance.

Investment Portfolio - Total investment holdings.

Investment Risk - The chance that the actual returns realized on an investment will differ from the expected return.

Investment Strategy - The method used to select which assets to include in a portfolio and to decide when to buy and sell those assets.

IRA Rollover - An individual may withdraw, tax-free, all or part of the assets from one IRA and reinvest them within sixty days into another IRA. A rollover of this type can occur only once in any one-year period. The one-year rule applies separately to each IRA that the individual owns. An individual must roll over into another IRA the same property that he or she received from the old IRA.

Junk Bonds - A bond that pays an unusually higher rate of return to compensate for a low credit rating.

Keogh - A tax-deferred retirement plan for self-employed individuals and employees of unincorporated businesses. A Keogh plan is similar to an IRA but with significantly higher contribution limits.

Leverage - Using leverage is the process of investing using borrowed funds. Leveraging investments can magnify returns, both positive and negative.

Life Expectancy - The average future time an individual can expect to live. Life expectancies have been increasing steadily over the past century and may continue to increase in the future.

Life Insurance - A contract between an individual and an insurance company that specifies that the insurer will provide either a stated sum or a periodic income to the individual's designated beneficiaries upon his or her death.

Life Settlement - This occurs when a person who does not have a terminal or chronic illness sells his or her life insurance policy to a third party for an amount that is less than the full amount of the death benefit. The buyer becomes the new owner or beneficiary of the life insurance policy, pays all future premiums, and collects the entire death benefit when the insured dies. Some states regulate the purchase as a security while others regulate it as insurance.

Lifetime Annuity - Lifetime annuities offer a way for an investor to receive a guaranteed income for the rest of his or her life, regardless of how long he or she lives. The income payments from the annuity will begin at a specific time. The amount of these payments is calculated based on the annuitant's life span as it is calculated by insurance company actuaries. Lifetime annuities offer an income stream that the annuitant cannot outlive.

Liquidity - The measure of one's ability to immediately turn assets into cash without penalty or risk of loss. Examples include a savings account, money market account, or checking account.

Living Benefit Annuity - These annuities can offer benefits prior to retirement time provided certain conditions are met, such as the annuity holder having a catastrophic or terminal illness. Different insurance companies have different rules with regard to how much money may be extracted from the annuity when receiving benefits early.

Living Will - If people become incapacitated, these documents will preserve his or her wishes and act as his or her voice in medical decisions.

Long Position - A long position in an investment indicates a current ownership in that investment that would increase in value as the underlying assets increase in value.

Margin - The amount of money supplied by an investor as a portion of the total funds needed to buy or sell a security, with the balance of required funds loaned to the investor by a broker, dealer, or other lender.

Margin Account - A special account set up by a broker for a client who wants to buy and sell securities using margin.

Margin Call - A call from a broker to a client asking for more money to back up a security purchased on margin when such a security has declined in value. If more money is not supplied, the broker usually sells the security.

Market Order - An order to buy at the lowest price going or sell at the highest price possible.

Market Risk - The risk that the entire market will decline, reducing an investment's value regardless of other factors.

Medical Power of Attorney - This special power of attorney allows an individual to designate another person to make medical decisions on his or her behalf.

Minimum Distributions - An individual must start receiving distributions from a qualified retirement plan by April 1 of the year following the year in which he or she reaches age seventy and a half. Subsequent distributions must occur by each December 31. The minimum distributions can be based on the life expectancy of the individual or the joint life expectancy of the individual and his or her- beneficiary.

Money Purchase Plan - A plan that has contributions that are a fixed percentage of compensation and are not based on the employer's profits.

Mortality - The risk of death of a given person based on factors such as age, health, gender, and lifestyle.

Municipal Bonds - A bond offered by a state, county, city, or other political entity such as a school district to raise public funds for special projects. The interest received from municipal bonds is often exempt from certain income taxes.

Mutual Funds - A mutual fund is a pooling of investor (shareholder) assets, which is professionally managed by an investment company for the benefit of the fund's shareholders. Each fund has specific investment objectives and associated risk. Mutual funds offer shareholders the advantage of diversification and professional management in exchange for a management fee.

MYGA (Multi Year Guaranteed) Annuity - This is a type of fixed annuity whereby the income payments to the annuitant are a guaranteed amount for more than one year.

Net Asset Value - The value of all the holdings of a mutual fund less the fund's liabilities.

Net Worth - The difference between an individual's total assets and total liabilities.

Note - A legal document that acknowledges a debt and the terms and conditions agreed upon by the borrower.

Odd Lot - An uneven number of securities that represents less than a board lot.

Offer Price - The price that a buyer is willing to pay for an investment.

Open-End Fund - A fund that continuously issues and redeems units, so the number of units outstanding varies from day to day. Most mutual funds are open-end funds. These are the opposite of closed-end funds.

Over-the-Counter (OTC) Market - Market created by dealer trading, as opposed to the auction market, which prevails on most major exchanges.

Paper Gain/Loss - Unrealized capital gain/loss on securities held in a portfolio, based on a comparison of current market price to original cost.

Par Bond - A bond that is selling at par.

Payroll Deduction - Payments made on behalf of an individual's employer. These payments are automatically deducted from the employee's paycheck.

Pension Annuity - When an individual retires from a company, he or she may have a choice of receiving either a pension annuity or a lump sum of cash from the pension plan. The pension annuity can be voluntarily contracted for by the individual, and it offers a stream of regular payments that are received by that former employee.

Period Certain Annuity - An annuity that will guarantee income payments for a specific period of time. Typically, the income is paid out to the annuitant until the specified time period ends. If the annuitant passes away during that period of time, the income will continue to be paid out to his or her beneficiary until the time period on the annuity has ended. Therefore, if the annuity holder had selected a fifteen-year time period, and he or she passes away after the eighth year, then the beneficiary will receive income from that annuity for an additional seven years.

Points - Charges that are added to a mortgage loan by the lender and are based on the loan amount. One point is equal to 1 percent of the original loan balance.

Policy - A contractual arrangement between an insurer and an insured that describes the terms and conditions of the insurance contract.

Policy Loan - A life insurance policy owner can borrow from the cash value component of many permanent insurance policies for virtually any purpose. Any policy loans that are outstanding at the time of death of the insured will be deducted from the benefits that are paid to the beneficiary.

Political Risk - The risk that stock prices may decline dramatically during periods of political unrest or crisis.

Power of Attorney - A legal document authorizing one person to act on behalf of another.

Premium - The payment that the owner of a life insurance policy makes to the insurer. In exchange for the premium payment, the insurer assumes the financial risk, as defined by the insurance policy, associated with the death of the insured.

Present Value - The current worth of a future payment, or stream of payments, discounted at a given interest rate over a given period of time.

Principal - The principal amount of a loan or mortgage is the outstanding balance, excluding interest.

Probate - The process used to make an orderly distribution and transfer of property from the deceased to a group of beneficiaries. The probate process is characterized by court supervision of property transfer, filing of claims against the estate by creditors, and publication of a last will and testament.

Profit Sharing Plan - The most flexible and simplest of the defined contribution retirement plans. It permits discretionary annual contributions that are generally allocated on the basis of compensation. The employer will determine the amount to be contributed each year depending on the cash flow of the company. The deduction for contributions to a profit sharing plan cannot be more than 15 percent of the compensation paid to the employees participating in the plan. Annual employer contributions to the account of a participant cannot exceed the smaller of $30,000 or 25 percent of a participant's compensation.

Prohibited IRA Transactions - Generally, a prohibited transaction is any improper (self-dealing) use of the IRA by the account owner. Some examples include borrowing money from an IRA, using an IRA to secure a loan, and selling property to an IRA.

Prospectus - A detailed statement prepared by an issuer and filed with the SEC prior to the sale of a new issue. The prospectus gives detailed information on the issue and on the issuer's condition and prospects.

Qualified Retirement Plan - A qualified retirement plan is a retirement plan that meets certain specified tax rules, contained primarily in Section 401(a) of the Internal Revenue Code. These rules are called plan qualification rules. If the rules are satisfied, the plan's trust is exempt from taxes.

Ratchet Annuity - A type of fixed index annuity. In this case, every year the account values in the annuity are reset, or ratcheted up, in order to include the gain for that particular year. Therefore, the principal that is in the annuity account is adjusted upward and will essentially form the new basis upon which the future participation calculations are made. In addition, in this case, the account value will never be adjusted downward, which assures the annuity holder that he or she will not have a loss of any principal.

Registered Representative - An individual who is licensed as a securities broker to act as an account representative for clients and collect commission income.

Rider - An amendment on an insurance policy that expands or restricts the policy's benefits.

Risk - Investment risk is the chance that the actual returns realized on an investment will differ from the expected return.

Rule of 72 - A way to determine the effect of compound interest. Divide 72 by the expected return on an investment. If the expected return is 8 percent, for example, assuming that all interest is reinvested, the investment will double in nine years.

Safety of Principal - An objective that emphasizes the security of the invested principal.

Salary Reduction Simplified Employee Pension (SARSEP) – A simplified alternative to a 401(k) plan. It is a SEP that includes a salary reduction arrangement. Under this special arrangement, eligible employees can elect to have the employer contribute part of his or her before-tax pay to the IRA. This amount is called an elective deferral.

Securities Exchange Commission (SEC) - The main regulatory body regulating the securities industry.

Securities - Stocks and bonds are traditionally referred to as securities. More specifically, stocks are often referred to as equities and bonds as debt instruments.

Short Position - A position in an investment that would increase in value as the underlying assets decrease in value; opposite of a long position.

Short Sale - The sale of stock that an investor does not yet own in order to take advantage of an expected share price decline. If the stock declines in price, the stock is purchased at the now lower price, and the short position is closed.

Simplified Employee Pension (SEP) - A simplified alternative to a qualified profit sharing plan. An SEP is essentially a written arrangement that allows an employer to make contributions toward his or her own and employees' retirement without becoming involved in a more complex retirement plan. Under an SEP, IRAs are not set up for each eligible employee. SEP contributions are made to IRAs of the participants in the plan. The employer has no control over the employee's IRA once the money is contributed.

Single Premium Fixed Annuity - With this type of annuity, the annuity holder makes one lump sum premium payment into the annuity contract. The income payments may begin either immediately or at a later time, depending upon the type of contract. The payments are fixed and thus guaranteed by the insurance company.

Single Premium Fixed Deferred Annuity - This annuity is purchased with one lump sum premium payment; however, the income benefits are deferred until a later time. These payments are a fixed amount and are guaranteed by the insurance company.

Single Premium Deferred Annuity (SPDA) - This type of annuity is purchased with one lump sum premium payment. The annuitant will not receive income payments until a time in the future. These annuities have two separate phases. These are the savings phase, when the funds in the account grow, and the income phase, when the annuitant receives income from the annuity.

Single Premium Immediate Annuity (SPIA) - SPIA annuities are purchased with a lump sum premium deposit, and then they typically will begin making regular monthly income payments to the annuitant.

Single Premium Variable Annuity - This annuity is funded with one lump sum premium payment. Income payments to the annuity holder may begin immediately or at some time in the future, depending upon whether the annuity is immediate or deferred. The income benefits to the annuitant will vary based upon market conditions and the underlying investment vehicles.

Single Premium Variable Deferred Annuity - This type of annuity is funded with one lump sum premium payment; however, the income benefits to the annuity holder will not begin until a time in the future. Because it is variable, the income payments will fluctuate based on underlying market conditions and the particular investment vehicles chosen.

Small Cap - A small cap stock is one issued by a company with less than $1.7 billion in market capitalization.

Spousal IRA - An individual can set up and contribute to an IRA for his or her spouse. This is called a spousal IRA, and it can be established if certain requirements are met. In the case of a spousal IRA, the individual and spouse must have separate IRAs. A jointly owned IRA is not permitted.

Stock - Stock certificates represent an ownership position in a corporation. Stockholders are often entitled to dividends, voting rights, and financial participation in company growth.

Stock Dividends - The investor's share of the income earned by the company issuing the stock.

Stock Exchange - A market for trading of equities, a public market for the buying and selling of public stocks.

Stop-Loss Order - When an investor tells his or her broker to sell a stock if it drops to a certain price.

Succession Planning - Planning for a business to pass to the next generation of owners or managers.

Surrender Value - When a policy owner surrenders his or her permanent life insurance policy to the insurance company, he or she receives the surrender value of that policy in return. The surrender value is the cash value of the policy plus any dividend accumulations, plus the cash value of any paid-up additions minus any policy loans, interest, and applicable surrender charges.

Tax Credit - An income tax credit directly reduces the amount of income tax paid by offsetting other income tax liabilities.

Tax Deduction - A reduction of total income before the amount of tax payable is calculated.

Tax-Deferred - The deferral of income taxes on interest earnings until the interest is withdrawn from the investment. Some vehicles or products that enjoy this special tax treatment include permanent life insurance, annuities, and any investment held in IRAs.

Technical Analysis - A technique of estimating a stock's future value strictly by examining its prices and volume of trading over time. Technical analysis is the opposite of fundamental analysis.

Term Insurance - Term insurance is life insurance coverage that pays a death benefit only if the insured dies within a specified period of time. Term policies do not have a cash value component and must be renewed periodically as dictated by the insurance contract.

Testamentary Trust - A trust created under the terms of a will and that takes effect upon the death of the testator.

Ticker Symbol - A combination of letters that identifies a stock exchange security.

Treasury Bill - Treasury bills, often referred to as T-bills, are short-term securities (with maturities of less than one year) offered and guaranteed by the federal government. They are issued at a discount and pay their full face value at maturity.

Treasury Bond - Treasury bonds are issued with maturities of more than ten years. These notes are offered and guaranteed by the U.S. government. They are issued at a discount and pay their full face value at maturity.

Treasury Note - Treasury notes are issued with maturities between one and ten years. These notes are offered and guaranteed by the U.S. government. They are issued at a discount and pay their full face value at maturity.

Tax-Sheltered Annuity - This type of annuity allows employees of public educational or other tax-exempt organizations to make pretax contributions through salary reduction into a tax-sheltered retirement plan. The employees are thus not taxed on the amount of the contribution until they begin making withdrawals at retirement. This term applies, for example, to a 403(b) plan.

Variable Annuity - A type of annuity that allows the annuity holder to allocate the premium dollars into different types of investments, or subaccounts. The value of these investments fluctuates based on market conditions and performance of those underlying investments.

Underwriter (banking) - A person, banker, or group that guarantees to furnish a definite sum of money by a definite date in return for an issue of bonds or stock.

Underwriter (insurance) - The person assuming a risk in return for the payment of a premium, or the person who assesses the risk and establishes premium rates.

Underwriter (investments) - In the bond/stock market, a brokerage firm or group of firms that has promised to buy a new issue of bonds/shares from a government or company at a fixed discounted price then arranges to resell them to investors at full price.

Universal Life Insurance - An adjustable universal life insurance policy provides both a death benefit and an investment component called a cash value. The cash value earns interest at rates dictated by the insurer. The policyholder may accumulate significant cash value over the years and, in some circumstances, "borrow" the appreciated funds without paying taxes on the borrowed gains (taxes may be required if the policy is surrendered). As long as the policy stays in force, the borrowed funds do not need to be repaid, but interest may be charged to the policyholder's cash value account. Premiums are adjustable by the policy owner.

Variable Deferred Annuity - A variable deferred annuity offers payments that are set to begin at some time in the future. The underlying investments in the contract are tied to market risks and can fluctuate in value.

Variable Investment - A variable investment is any investment whose value, and therefore returns, fluctuates with market conditions such as a common stock, a plot of raw land, or a hard asset.

Variable Universal Life Insurance - A life insurance policy that provides both a death benefit and an investment component called a cash value. The owner of the policy invests the cash value in subaccounts selected by the insurer. The policyholder may accumulate significant cash value over the year and "borrow" the appreciated funds without paying taxes on the borrowed gains (taxes may be required if the policy is surrendered). As long as the policy stays in force, the borrowed funds do not need to be repaid, but interest may be charged to the cash value account.

Vesting - The law requires that a qualified plan have a schedule under which a participant earns an ownership interest in employer-provided contributions based on his or her years of service with the employer. Amounts contributed by the participant are always 100 percent vested.

Viatical Settlement - Occurs when a person with a terminal or chronic illness sells his or her life insurance policy to a third party for an amount that is less than the full amount of the death benefit. The buyer becomes the new owner or beneficiary of the policy, pays all future premiums, and collects the entire death benefit when the insured dies. Some states regulate the purchase as a security while others regulate it as insurance.

Waiver of Premium - A waiver of premium rider on an insurance policy sets conditions under which premium payments are not required to be made on time. The most popular waiver of premium rider is the disability waiver, under which the owner of the policy is not required to make premium payments during a period of total disability.

Whole-Life Insurance - A traditional whole-life insurance policy provides both a death benefit and a cash value component. The policy is designed to remain in force for a lifetime. Premiums stay level, and the death benefit is guaranteed. Over time, the cash value of the policy grows and helps keep the premium level. Although the premium starts out significantly higher than that of a comparable term life policy, over time the level premium eventually is overtaken by the ever-increasing premium of a term policy.

Wrap Account - An account offered by investment dealers whereby investors are charged an annual management fee based on the value of invested assets.

Yield - The yield on an investment is the total proceeds paid from the investment and is calculated as a percentage of the amount invested.

Zero-Coupon Bond - A zero-coupon bond is a bond sold without interest-paying coupons. Instead of paying periodic interest, the bond is sold at a discount and pays its entire face amount upon maturity, which is usually a one-year period or longer.

INDEX

"annuity" is defined · **48**

403(b) · **56**, **227**, **250**

A

Advisor Screening Process · **190**

annuities – just like any other investment · **47**

Annuities & Estate Tax · **169**

Annuities & Retirement · **168**

Annuities and Tax · **162**

annuities are not necessarily · **51**

Annuities Attacked · **211**, **218**

annuities can be annuitized · **50**

Annuities can be funded · **50**

Annuity History · **65**

Annuity Satisfaction · **162**

annuity withdrawal · **50**, **167**

Are Annuities Safe · **156**

Average · 131

average index monthly earnings (AIME) · 222

Avoiding Scams · **200**

B

Best Fixed Annuity · **70**

Best Variable Annuities · **87**

Blend · 132

Bonus Annuity · **57**, **229**

Broker/Dealers · 31

brokercheck · 33, 199, 203

C

Cap · 130

Capped Monthly Sum or Average · 132

Captive Agent · 36

Cash account · 183

Certain Period · **53**, **112**

Certain Period Annuity · **53**

CFP – Certified Financial Planner · **37**

Check Out Brokers and Investment Advisors · **198**

ChFC – Chartered Financial Consultant · **37**

COLA · **50**, **111**, **113**, **117**

COLA SPIA · **113**

Commission · 31, 194, 195, 231, 247

commission basis · 35

Comprehensive Social Security planning · 225

conflict of interest · 32, 42

contractual guarantees. · 129

court order process · 179

Critics of annuities · **64**

CSA – Certified Senior Advisor · **38**

D

Death Benefit Riders · **139**

deferral aspect of annuities · **51**

Deferred annuities · **51**

disclosure · 35, 36, 190, 196, 200

Diversification · 179

Division of Corporate Finance · **196**

Division of Enforcement · **196**

Division of Investment Management · **196**

Division of Market Regulation · **196**

E

Ethics for Advisors · **187**

Exclusion Ratio · **115**

F

Factoring companies · 181

Fee Based · 35

Fee Only · 32, 35

Fee-Based · 32

Fee-Offset · 32

Fees · 132

FIA's & Hybrids · **174**

fiduciary · 31, 35, 36, 39, 42, 188

Fiduciary · 36, 236

File and suspend · 223

FINRA · 33, 193, 195, 202, 203, 204, 212

Fixed Annuities · **53, 68, 88, 157, 163**

Fixed Annuity Alternatives · **75**

Fixed Annuity Benefits · **68**

Fixed Annuity CD Style · **74**

Fixed Annuity Characteristics · **69**

Fixed Annuity Performance · **70**

Fixed Deferred Annuity Characteristics · **73**

Fixed Index Annuity Features · **96**

Fixed Index Annuity or **Equity Indexed Annuity** · 55

Fixed Index Annuity Performance · **103**

Fixed Index Deferred Annuity · **55, 236**

flat fee · 32

flexibility · 183

Flexible Premium Fixed Annuity · **54, 236**

Flexible Premium Fixed Deferred Annuity, · **54**

Flexible Premium Variable Deferred Annuity · **57, 237**

Fraternal Annuity · **56, 237**

full retirement age (FRA) · 222

future income needs · **49, 50**

G

Gift Annuity · **56, 238**

Great Depression · **65**

Great Recession · 30

growth in deferral · 129

guaranteed income · **50, 52, 62, 68, 84, 97, 142, 154, 163, 242**

Guaranteed Interest Contract Annuities (GICs) · **55**

H

High Yields · 179

Hourly-Rate · 32

Hybrid annuities · 134

Hybrid Annuity Benefits · **128**

Hybrid Annuity Disadvantages · **133**

Hybrid Annuity Features · **125**

I

Immediate Annuity · **52, 110, 111, 114, 116, 117, 118, 239, 248**

Immediate Annuity Benefits · **114**

Immediate Annuity Disadvantages · **117**

Immediate Annuity Features · **111**

Immediate Annuity Performance · **116**

Important Questions an Expert · **40**

Important Questions to Ask · **39**

income account · 129

Income Annuity · **53, 239**

Income Rider · 129

Income Rider Fees · 183

Increasing Payout Option · **150**

Independent Agent · **36**

Index Annuity · **54, 55, 96, 98, 103, 104, 236, 239**

Index Annuity History · **96**

Individual Retirement Annuity · **58, 240**

inflation · **49, 50, 62, 83, 84, 85, 92, 109, 111**, 117, **122, 126, 128, 133, 134, 151, 154, 187**

Inflation Protection · **111**

Initial Premium · 129

Insurance Agent · 34

insurance company actuaries · **52, 242**

Investment Advisor Representative · 35

investment management fees · 35

Irrevocable Contracts · **118**

J

Joint and Survivor · **113**

joint payout · 129

L

Life Only · **112**

Life with Cash Refund · **113**

Life with Installment Refund · **113**

Life with Period Certain (or Certain and Life) · **112**

Lifetime Annuities · **52**

liquidity · 183

Living Benefit Annuity · **57, 242**

Living Benefit Riders · **142**

lock in gains · **64**

long term retirement plan · **51**

---

long-term fixed annuity · **51**

lump sum · **50, 51, 52, 53, 54, 57, 73, 108, 109**, 111, **113, 127, 141, 165, 166, 228, 239, 244, 248**

M

majority control · 129

MYGA (Multi Year Guaranteed Annuity) or CD Type Annuity · 56

N

National Ethics Bureau · **40, 215**

negative press for years about Social Security's demise · 219

no surrender or penalty charge · 129

non-market correlated asset · 179

O

Old Age Benefits · 222

or lump sum payments · 182

P

Participation · 131

penalty free withdrawals · **63**

Pension Annuity · 53, 244

Period Certain Immediate Annuity · 52

Predictable future income · 182

Pre-Issued Annuities ™ · 179, 181

primary insurance amount (PIA) · 222

Protection from Creditors · **115**

Protection from Medicaid · **115**

R

Ratchet Annuity · **55, 246**

Refund, Liquidity, and Withdrawal Options · **111**

Registered Investment Advisor · 13, 35, 36, 212

Registered Representative · 31, 34, 36, 246

Registered Representatives · 31, 34, 36

regulatory agencies · 33

required quotas · **39**

retirement allocation. · **62**

Rollovers & Annuities · **171**

S

Safety · 179, 182

Sales quotas · 31

Same sex marriage partners · 222

Securities and Exchange Commission (SEC) · **195**

securities exam · 33

Security entitled US citizen · 219

Series 65 · 35, 212

single payout · 129

Single Premium Fixed Annuity · **54, 248**

Single Premium Fixed Deferred Annuity · **54, 248**

Single Premium Variable Deferred Annuity · **57, 248**

Social Security is doomed · 218

Social Security optimization · 226

Social Security was designed to function · 221

Social Security, let's list some of the interesting factors · 222

Social Security's probability of remaining viable · 218

Solicitor · 34

SPDA (Single Premium Deferred) · **52**

SPIA (Single Premium Immediate) · **52**

Split Annuity Combo · **114**

Spread · 130

state guarantee insurance association (SIGA) · **75**

Stock Broker · 34

suitability · 31, 33

Surrender fees · 183

survivor benefits · 224

T

Tax Sheltered Annuity · **56**, **250**

ten percent IRS penalty · **63**, **78**, **172**, **176**

Things to Consider · **104**

topping off · 224

Trader Vic Index · 135

TVI Index · 135

Types of Living Benefit Riders · **144**

U

Uncapped Index · 130

V

Variable Annuity · **56, 57, 84, 85, 86, 88, 89, 237, 248, 250**

Variable Annuity Alternatives · **88**

Variable Annuity Benefits · **86**

Variable Annuity Disadvantages · **89**

Variable Annuity Features · **85**

Variable Deferred Annuity · **57, 251**

Variable Payments · **112**

W

What Are Annuity Riders · **139**

Y

Your Responsibilities · **43**

Further Disclosure

The Dow Jones Industrial Average is a price-weighted index of 30 actively traded blue-chip stocks. The NASDAQ Composite Index is an unmanaged, market-weighted index of all over-the-counter common stocks traded on the National Association of Securities Dealers Automated Quotation System. The Standard & Poor's 500 (S&P 500) is an unmanaged group of securities considered to be representative of the stock market in general. It is not possible to invest directly in an index. NYSE Group, Inc. (NYSE:NYX) operates two securities exchanges: the New York Stock Exchange (the "NYSE") and NYSE Arca (formerly known as the Archipelago Exchange, or ArcaEx®, and the Pacific Exchange). NYSE Group is a leading provider of securities listing, trading and market data products and services. The New York Mercantile Exchange, Inc. (NYMEX) is the world's largest physical commodity futures exchange and the preeminent trading forum for energy and precious metals, with trading conducted through two divisions - the NYMEX Division, home to the energy, platinum, and palladium markets, and the COMEX Division, on which all other metals trade. All information is believed to be from reliable sources; however we make no representation as to its completeness or accuracy. All economic and performance data is historical and not indicative of future results. Market indices discussed are unmanaged. Investors cannot invest in unmanaged indices. The publisher is not engaged in rendering legal, accounting or other professional services. If other expert assistance is needed, the reader is advised to engage the services of a competent professional. Please consult your Financial Advisor for further information. Additional risks are associated with international investing, such as currency fluctuations, political and economic instability and differences in accounting standards.